FLAGS AT SEA

Flags at Sea

A guide to the flags flown at sea by ships of the major maritime nations, from the 16th century to the present day, illustrated from the collections of the National Maritime Museum.

Timothy Wilson

NATIONAL MARITIME MUSEUM

&

CHATHAM PUBLISHING

LONDON

Text © Crown copyright 1986. Reproduced with the permission of the Controller of Her Majesty's Stationery Office

Photographs © National Maritime Museum

This edition published 1999 by the National Maritime Museum in association with Chatham Publishing, 61 Frith Street, London W1V 5TA. Chatham Publishing is an imprint of the Duckworth Media Group

British Library cataloguing in Publication Data
A catalogue record for this book is available from the British Library

ISBN 1 86176 116 3

Page 32: The National Maritime Museum wishes to thank Mr Rodney Wilkinson for kind permission to reproduce 'The Royal Yacht Britannia at Greenwich, 1954' by Norman Wilkinson, © Rodney Wilkinson, 1999

Appendix B is reproduced by kind permission of the Navy Records Society.
Additions to Bibliography by Barbara Tomlinson

Printed in China by Midas Printing Limited

Contents

		page
Abbreviations		6
List of illustrations		7
Preface		8
Introduction		9
1.	Flags of the British Navy	12
2.	Flags of British Ships other than the Royal Navy	33
3.	Sea Flags of the United States of America	47
4.	Some Sea Flags of Europe:	
	Spain	53
	The Netherlands	56
	France	60
5.	Flag Signalling	77
6.	The Manufacture of Sea Flags	85
7.	The Flag Collection at the National Maritime Museum	89

Appendices
A. Accounts for flags supplied to the *Henri Grace à Dieu*, 1514 — 93

	page
B. Nathaniel Boteler's discussion of flags	95
C. A proclamation concerning colours to be worn on board ships, 1694	97
D. 'Of Colours', from *Regulations and Instructions Relating to His Majesty's Service at Sea* (1731)	98
E. Order in Council of 9 July 1864, abolishing the use of squadronal colours in the Royal Navy	99
Notes	100
Glossary	108
Classified bibliography	
A. Flag books and flag charts up to 1860 (by date)	113
B. Flag books and general works (1860 to the present)	115
C. British flags	116
D. Flags of some other nations (alphabetically, by country)	117
E. House flags	119
F. Miscellaneous	120
Index	121

Abbreviations

BL	British Library
FB	*Flag Bulletin*
MM	*Mariner's Mirror*
NMM	National Maritime Museum
NRS	Navy Records Society
OED	*Oxford English Dictionary*
Pepys MS	Magdalene College Cambridge, Pepys Manuscripts
PRO	Public Record Office
RUSI	Royal United Services Institute (formerly Royal United Service Institution)

List of Illustrations

Colour plates

I-III   British flags
IV   a. Flag drawings from William Down-
           man's notebook (1685-6)
V   'The Spanish Armada in the English
           Channel, 1588' (anon. gouache, c.1610)
VI   Flag chart published by B. Lens (c. 1700)
VII   Union flag from the *Queen Charlotte*
           (1794)
VIII   Flag chart published by R.H. Laurie
           (1842)
IX   'The Relief of Barcelona, 1706' (oil
           painting by H. Vale)
X   'The Battle of Camperdown, 1797'
           (oil painting by Thomas Whitcombe)
XI   English command flag c. 1652-4
XII   Armorial banner of Frederick, Duke
           of York and Albany (c. 1790-1800)
XIII   Command flag of the Dutch Vice
           Admiral de Winter (1797)
XIV-XVI   American and European flags

Preface

This book presents some of the material for the history of sea flags in the incomparable collections of the National Maritime Museum. It is not a comprehensive book of 'flags of the world', and I have tried to avoid duplicating the sort of information on present-day flags that is readily available in books such as Barraclough and Crampton's excellent *Flags of the World*. Apart from Great Britain, I have dealt in the text only with the flags of the four countries whose maritime history is most closely linked to Britain's – Spain, the Netherlands, France, and the United States. However, the flag charts in Plates IV, VI and VIII, which are reproduced here for the first time, should help the identification of other flags in paintings, and the Bibliography includes a selection of publications on flags of other European countries.

All the photographs are of items in the collections of the National Maritime Museum and are the work of the Museum's photographic studio. The flag drawings are by Lionel Willis.

I owe a debt of gratitude to the Trustees, Director and staff of the National Maritime Museum for support in many ways, and to Neil Stratford, Keeper of Medieval & Later Antiquities at the British Museum, for encouragement to complete the book after my move to his department. I am also grateful to the staff of the British Library and the Naval Historical Library for help and advice.

I have received indispensable help and information from friends, colleagues, and correspondents in Great Britain and abroad. Among many, I am particularly grateful to Teddy Archibald, Pat Billings, Bridget Clifford, William Crampton, Alice S. Creighton, Ian Friel, Lynne Friel, Margaret George, Jacky Hayton, Sebastián Herreros Agüí, David Joyce, John Munday, Richard Nelson, Lt. Cdr. Frans van Oosten, Georges Pasch, Ann Payne, Alan Pearsall, R.G. Porter, Rina Prentice, David Proctor, Michael Robinson, Natalie Rothstein, Klaes Sierksma, Whitney Smith, Lt. Cdr. Felix Thorpe, Barbara Tomlinson, and R.E.J. Weber. The mistakes are my own.

Introduction

The flags used by ships are the heraldry and the traditional language of the sea. For centuries flags were the only form of communication between ships out of hailing distance of one another, and between ships and the shore, and the language of flags was developed to express several different kinds of information.[1] A modern British ensign does not only announce the British nationality of the ship wearing it; it also reveals whether it is part of the Royal Navy, on other public business, or privately owned. A merchant ship's house flag indicates the owners, a naval command flag the rank of the officer in command, a yacht's burgee the club to which the owner belongs. Signalling with special signal flags developed in the 19th century into a system capable of passing elaborate messages between any two ships, even if the crews had no common language,

and is even now not obsolete. On special occasions flags can be used purely for decorative and festive effect. On the other hand, a ship's colours, like those of a regiment, are the symbols of its honour and identity, and naval history has its share of tales of heroic deeds 'to keep the colours flying'.

This range of functions in flags which are generally of relatively simple design sets the study of sea flags somewhat apart from that of land flags and of heraldry in general. Significantly, although English uses the word 'flag' equally at sea and on land, there are several languages that recognize a distinction and have separate words: a French ship has *pavillons*, not *drapeaux*; and a German ship has *Flaggen*, not *Fahnen*.

Although city and provincial flags in Great Britain do not have the importance that they have in

1 H.M. Frigate *Cambrian*, after J.T. Serres, 1805 (from *Liber Nauticus*)

countries such as Germany or the Netherlands, the range of British sea flags is uniquely complex. There is a glossary of terms on pp.108-12, but it may be useful to summarize here the terminology of the most common types of sea flag.

Pennant

The term 'pennant' can be used for any long tapering flag: the masthead pennant which is the mark of a naval vessel in commission, is long and narrow; the broad pennants of naval commodores are swallow-tailed; the pennants of the International Code of Signals are blunt ended; name pennants and pennants used for other more or less unofficial purposes come in various shapes and sizes.

Flag of Command

The flag of a 'flag officer' (i.e. of the rank of rear admiral or above). A flag of command is hoisted instead of a commissioning pennant when the flag officer is aboard his ship.

Royal Standard

The flag of the sovereign, consisting of the royal arms, is generally known as the Royal Standard, though heraldic purists prefer to call it the Royal Banner. The development of the Royal Standard of Great Britain is shown in Plate I, nos. 1-8.

House Flag

Since the first half of the 19th century it has been customary for merchant ships to fly a private flag of the owner, whether a company or an individual, and these flags are known as 'house flags'.

Ensign

The ensign, traditionally placed at the stern of a ship, is the principal identifying national flag of warships and merchant ships.

Jack

A jack is the flag worn at a jackstaff in the bows of a ship; it is normally smaller than the ensign. In strict usage 'Union Jack' is a term used only for the small version worn at the bows of a Royal Navy ship; when flown elsewhere at sea, or on land, it is called the 'Union Flag'. At sea the Union Jack and the Union Flag are confined by law to Royal Navy vessels, although on land the Union Flag is the national flag of the United Kingdom and may be used by anyone.

The history of the varied flags used by British and other ships reflects political, dynastic and heraldic developments over several centuries. Their use at sea has been affected by the evolution of naval tactics, the conditions of seaborne trade, and the technology of ship design and communications, so that the history of sea flags is inseparable from general maritime history. Anyone who wants to find out what flags were used by a particular ship on a particular occasion will usually have to seek the answer in contemporary historical sources: a book of 'Flags of the World', even if it is accurate (which few before the middle of the 19th century are), is unlikely to provide an adequate answer. It is part of the purpose of this book to give ship modellers and marine artists an idea of the kind of source material that exists, as well as to provide a guide to the flags in old marine paintings.

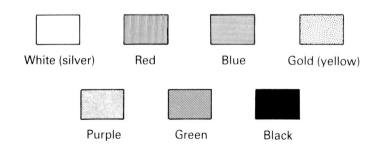

White (silver)   Red   Blue   Gold (yellow)

Purple   Green   Black

2 Colour coding system for line illustrations

Any history of the flags flown by British ships rests largely on the detailed documentary research done by W.G. Perrin, then Admiralty Librarian, for his *British Flags*, published in 1922, which remains indispensable for the official documentation it contains. However, it can rarely be assumed that the ships on any historical occasion flew the theoretically 'correct' flags, so that evidence from official records has to be supplemented by contemporary narrative sources and visual evidence. It is not uncommon to find evidence of one kind contradicting that of another. The evidence of paintings is particularly hard to assess: some artists are consistently careful and reliable about details of flags; for example, the two Willem Van de Veldes, who were virtually the first professional marine painters to make a point of technical accuracy, or professional seamen like Nicholas Pocock (1741-1821). But there are many artists whose works are worthless as evidence; and even in the work of the 'professionals' a distinction has to be drawn between paintings and drawings of scenes they actually witnessed and works done later.

The history of sea flags is not a cut-and-dried subject: there are still many problems unsolved and many pictures unexplained. The National Maritime Museum contains in books and manuscripts, in pictures and drawings, and in its collection of historic flags, a rich body of source material in which many discoveries are still to be made, and of which only a small sample can be given here.

Two conventions have been adopted in the illustrations, both of them derived from heraldry. One is a system of colour coding (Fig. 2) for line illustrations, based on the so-called Petra Sancta system, which is named after a Jesuit writer on heraldry of the 17th century. The other is the convention by which flags are drawn with the 'hoist' to the reader's left and the 'fly' to his right.

CHAPTER 1

Flags of the British Navy

In April 1514 the *Henri Grace à Dieu*, the new pride of the young Henry VIII's fleet, was supplied with a splendid new set of flags, for which detailed invoices survive (App.A). One batch was supplied in April by John Brown, 'the King's painter'. The first item was an enormous streamer for the main masthead, 51 yards (46.6 metres) long 'and the breadth according'; a second streamer was 20 yards (18.3 metres) long. For use at deck level there were ten armorial banners three and a half yards (3.2 metres) long, and a further ten three yards (2.7 metres) long, all decorated with gold and silver and fringed with silk. The larger ones were priced at two pounds two shillings each, the smaller, at two pounds. The more basic white flags with the red cross of St George, of which ten were provided, cost only tenpence each. A few weeks later, Vincenzo Volpe, an Italian painter working in England, delivered a second consignment consisting of several streamers bearing beasts used as supporters to the royal arms (a dragon, a greyhound and a lion), two little streamers with the cross of St George, a hundred of the small pennants called 'pencels', and fifty more banners. His total bill, after haggling, came to £112. 19s. 8d.[2]

The *Henri Grace a Dieu*, was exceptionally lavishly equipped, but the types of flag in this list are characteristic of those used on the king's ships at the time. The cross of St George had been the principal emblem of England since the 14th century and was common as a flag in itself and as an element in the elaborate heraldic standards of the king and nobility: it was then, as now, the national flag of England (Plate I, no. 10). In Scotland the white saltire of St Andrew occupied a similar position (Plate I, no. 11). The royal arms and badges were the personal emblems of the sovereign and were the main devices used on the king's ships. The royal arms had been since about 1407 the three gold fleurs-de-lis on blue of France quartering the three gold lions on red of England (Plate I, no. 1). The badges used by Henry VIII included rose, portcullis, fleur-de-lis and (for

Queen Katherine of Aragon) pomegranate.[3]

The masthead streamers, by far the largest flags in the accounts, were particularly popular for royal ships in the reign of Henry VIII. Figure 3 is taken from a Tudor painting of Henry VIII setting off for the 'Field of the Cloth of Gold' in 1520: the mastheads are festooned with streamers with St George's cross. This lavish use of large streamers, particularly on royal ships and to mark special occasions, lasted into the 17th century.[4] In addition to these displays of banners and streamers, ships of the 15th and early 16th centuries were sometimes decorated with displays of armorial shields (pavises) along the bulwarks and with decoration on sails.[5]

Medieval ships, particularly ones which were named after a saint, often had flags with pictures of saints or with the coats of arms that contemporary heralds fancifully ascribed to them.[6] In the 1530s and 1540s the cult of the saints came under fire from Protestant criticism of 'superstitious images' and the images of saints and their supposed arms disappeared from flags.[7] Only the 'cross of St George', which had come to be seen as a national, rather than a religious emblem, survived.[8] From the reign of Elizabeth I English sea flags tend to be predominantly geometrical or heraldic rather than representational. There was no English equivalent to the procession of saints which decorated the flags of the Spanish Armada.

Figure 4, another 18th-century engraving, after a now destroyed Tudor painting of the battle off Portsmouth in 1545 between the English and the French fleets (the battle during which the *Mary Rose* was lost) shows the *Henri Grace à Dieu* some thirty years after she received her first set of flags. As the flagship she is distinguished by Royal Standards at the bow and stern and by a large streamer at the main. The other English ships fly various pennants, flags of St George and striped flags.[9]

Flags at the masthead were already used in the Middle Ages to mark out the flagship of the

THE EMBARKATION OF KING HENRY VIII AT DOVER MAY XXXI.ST MDXX.
PREPARATORY TO HIS INTERVIEW WITH THE FRENCH KING FRANCIS I.

3

4 The English fleet at the Battle of Portsmouth, 1545 (after a destroyed Tudor painting)

commander-in-chief of a fleet, but there is little evidence before the reign of Henry VIII on how this was done in the English navy. In 1530 a set of orders drawn up by Thomas Audley laid down that 'the Admiral ought to have this order before he joins battle with the enemy that all his ships shall bear a flag in their mizzen tops and himself one in the foremast beside [i.e. as well as] the mainmast, that every one may know his own fleet by that token'.[10] The more sophisticated tactics adopted towards the end of Henry VIII's reign involved dividing the fleet into squadrons distinguished by the position of their masthead flags, with each of the flagships having an extra flag. In the orders issued by the Lord Admiral, John Dudley, Viscount Lisle, on 10 August 1545 the fleet was divided into the van, the centre (commanded by the Lord Admiral), and the wing: the Lord Admiral flew the Royal Standard at the main and the flag of St George at the fore; the admiral of the van squadron flew flags of St George at main and

13

5 Drake's attack on the Spanish settlement at San Augustin, 1586, from a contemporary engraving. Note the similarity of the shipboard ensigns and those carried by the soldiers

fore; and the admiral of the wing squadron flew flags of St George at the mizzen and bonaventure mizzen. The other ships flew a single flag of St George at main, fore or mizzen, according to their squadron.[11] A fleet of 1558, under the command of William Wynter, was organized more simply: the admiral and vice admiral flew flags at the main and fore respectively, while all other warships in the fleet had a flag of St George at the bonaventure mizzen.[12]

The characteristic flag of the reigns of Elizabeth I and James I was the striped ensign, which developed out of the striped deck level flags used on the ships of Henry VIII's navy. Both the word 'ensign' (of which a 16th-century variant was 'ancient') and the use of striped flags seem to have originated in military use; the earliest sea ensigns were mounted on deck and removable, staff and all, for use on land.[13] By the end of the century striped stern ensigns were common on European ships and those of English ships were often distinguished by a cross of St George in a canton or overall (Figs. 6a, 6c).[14] To judge from the scattered evidence of illustrations, the colours of ensigns varied from ship to ship: although red and white (the colours of the cross of St George) and green and white (the Tudor livery colours) were used, there seems sometimes to have been no significance in the colours chosen.

Inventories of the royal ships that fought against the Spanish Armada in 1588 make it clear that they each had an ensign, but do not record the colours. In addition, flags of St George are listed for every ship, and most had streamers. There is also mention of pennants 'to discern their company from the enemy'.[15] Many of the ships in the fleet were privately owned and their flags may not have conformed to any completely consistent pattern.

The *Ark Royal*, flagship of the Lord Admiral, Howard of Effingham, flew at the main a flag with the royal arms which near-contemporary portrayals variously show as a Royal Standard (with the coat of arms occupying the entire flag) or with the full achievement of arms, with royal cypher and supporters, on a plain or striped field, as well as a flag of St George, an ensign, streamers and pennants. There may too, have been a banner of Howard's own arms (Fig. 8).[16] An account of the Armada by Petruccio Ubaldino, an Italian who was living in England, includes a passage which gives an impression of the ceremonial attached to the flags of command in the fleet.

The Lord Admiral, on his arrival at Plymouth, whither he had been ordered by the Queen to join up with Sir Francis Drake, proceeded in battle order, flying on the mast of his flagship the Royal Standard and also on a suitable place on the same ship the Standard of the Vice Admiral, already appointed to his office by the Queen. Before his arrival Sir Francis Drake, who had until then been Admiral in those parts, sailed out of the harbour to meet him with his 30 ships in orderly file of 3 lines . . . A salute was fired and it was followed by friendly applause on both sides, the artillery being accompanied by the trumpets and drums and by the joyful cheering of the ships' companies. Then Sir Francis Drake, out of respect to the rank and dignity of the office and in honour of the Lord Admiral, who was already close by, lowered his own Admiral's standard to pay tribute to Lord Howard, from whose ship, on his orders, the Vice Admiral's flag was taken down and sent as a gift to Drake, who was thus able to use it as his own from that moment. . . Thereupon Sir Francis Drake, lowering his former standard from its place, hoisted the new one just received, with military ceremonial, showing a suitable deference as befitted their respective ranks.[17]

There are a number of paintings and engravings of the *Ark Royal* and the battle, including Plate V, but none of them is of much authority for the flags. The professional marine painter who makes sure he gets such details right was not yet on the scene.[18]

A few years after the Armada, in 1596, an English fleet was sent out under the command of Howard and the Earl of Essex to attack Cadiz. The fleet was divided into four squadrons, each with three flag officers, and some surviving drawings of the flags used on the expedition show that flags similar to the striped ensigns of the period were used as flags of command. The basis of the elaborate system of distinction adopted was that an admiral's command flag was flown at the main masthead, a vice admiral's at the fore, and a rear admiral's at the mizzen: this was a guiding principle for the arrangement of admirals' flags in the British navy (and other

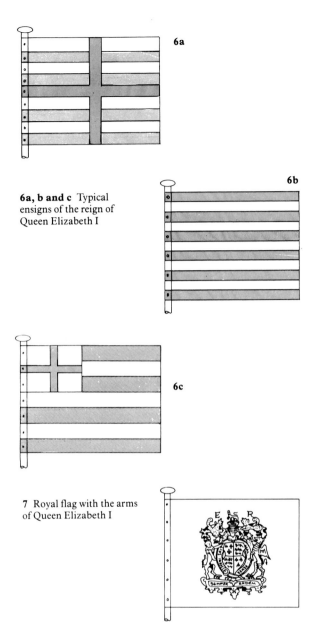

6a, b and c Typical ensigns of the reign of Queen Elizabeth I

7 Royal flag with the arms of Queen Elizabeth I

European navies) until the decline of the three-masted sailing warship in the 19th century. Howard in the *Ark Royal*, for instance, flew the Royal Standard at the main (together with a flag of St George at the fore), while the vice and rear admirals of his squadron flew a flag striped red/white/blue/red/white/blue/red, with St George's cross in a canton, at the fore and mizzen respectively.[19]

The accession in 1603 of James VI of Scotland to the English throne as James I, brought about a permanent union of the crowns of the two countries. The new Royal Standard quartered the Tudor arms

8 Impression of the seal of Lord Howard of Effingham, the matrix dated 1585; his arms are represented on the ship's sail

George with a border taken from its white field over the cross of St Andrew (Plate I, no. 12). This design, which gave the English cross precedence over the Scottish, was only chosen after some argument. An earlier pattern of 'Union' flag arranged the crosses of St George and St Andrew quarterly (Fig. 9a).[20] The design adopted in 1606 proved understandably unpopular north of the Border and a protest was sent to the King in August 1606, but to no avail: the official design was not changed. Scottish hostility to

9a

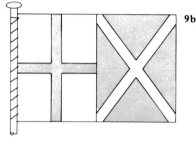

9b

9a and b Two early Stuart variant designs of the Union Flag

of England with the lion of Scotland and a harp to represent Ireland (Plate I, no. 2). Wales was, and remains, a principality belonging to the Prince of Wales, and has never been represented in the British Royal Standard. (An escutcheon of the arms of Wales is included in the Standard of the Prince of Wales). Three years later was designed the flag that was to become the symbol of the United Kingdom. On 12 April 1606, the King issued 'A proclamation declaring what Flags South and North Britains shall bear at Sea':

Whereas some difference hath arisen betweene our Subiects of South and North Britaine travayling by Seas, about the bearing of their Flagges: For the avoyding of all such contentions hereafter, Wee have with the advise of our Councell ordered; That from henceforth all our Subiects of this Isle and Kingdome of great Britaine, and the members thereof, shall beare in their Maintoppe the Red Crosse, commonly called S. Georges Crosse, and the White Crosse commonly called S. Andrewes Crosse, joyned together, according to a forme made by our Heralds, and sent by us to our Admirall to bee published to our said Subiects: And in their Fore-toppe our Subiects of South Britaine, shall weare the Red Crosse only as they were wont, and our Subiects of North Britaine in their Fore-toppe the White Crosse onely as they were accustomed. Wherefore we will and command all our Subiects to be conformable and obedient to this our Order, and that from henceforth they doe not use to beare their Flagges in any other sort, as they will answere the contrary at their perill.

The design adopted for this 'British Flag', or 'Union Flag' as it came to be called, placed the cross of St

the design persisted, and there is evidence in the 17th and 18th centuries of the use of a 'Scotch Union Flag', in which St Andrew's cross was placed on top of St George's (Fig. 10).[21] Alternative patterns were also sometimes used on English vessels: a quarterly pattern was used by Prince Charles in 1623, and an impaled pattern (Fig. 9b) on Royalist ships in 1643.[22]

The Union Flag was originally designed for general use at sea, as a way of denoting the common allegiance of Englishmen and Scots to one king.[23] In 1634, however, Charles I issued a new proclamation by which the right to fly the Union was restricted to the king's own ships:

Wee taking into Our Royall consideration that it is meete for the Honour of Our owne Ships in Our Navie Royall and of such other Ships as are or shall be employed in Our immediate Service, that the same bee by their Flags distinguished from the ships of any other of Our Subiects, doe hereby straitly prohibite and forbid

10 Scottish flags, from a signal book of 1756 (Bibl. A 22); the field of the ensign is red

that none of Our Subjects, of any of Our Nations and Kingdomes, shall from henceforth presume to carry the Union Flagge in the maine toppe, or other part of any of their Ships . . . but that the same Union Flagge bee still reserved as an ornament proper for Our owne Ships and Ships in Our immediate Service and Pay, and none other . . .

In future, the proclamation continued, privately owned English ships were to revert to flying St George's cross as a national flag, and Scottish ships St Andrew's cross.[24]

The restriction of the Union to the king's ships was linked to Charles I's attempts to restore the power of the 'Navie Royall', which had not been maintained under James I. It was in particular the outcome of disputes over an issue that loomed large in 17th-century naval affairs, the so-called 'Right of the Flag'. Since the Middle Ages the kings of England had claimed sovereignty over the 'Narrow Seas' between England and the Continent. All foreign ships were required to acknowledge this sovereignty by lowering flags and topsails in salute to any ship belonging to the English Crown. Charles I and his admirals were anxious to enforce this 'right', and there consequently had to be a visible distinction between the king's ships and others.[25] In 1634 the Union was made the distinctive flag of the navy, and it has been illegal for other ships to fly it without special permission ever since.

11 H.C. Vroom, 'The *Prince Royal* with Prince Charles returning from Spain 1623' (detail)

The form in which the king's ships came to fly the Union was a jack, a small flag, generally of rather square proportions, on a flagstaff rigged on the bowsprit. A larger version was used at the mastheads as a command flag.[26]

In the reign of James I striped stern ensigns remained popular. The National Maritime Museum painting by H.C. Vroom of the *Prince Royal* and the fleet that accompanied Prince Charles on the return voyage from the expedition to woo the Spanish *Infanta* in 1623 (Fig. 11) shows all the ships in the

12 The *Sovereign of the Seas*, engraved by J. Payne; a fully decked-out English flagship of the years before the Civil War

fleet with ensigns with St George's cross in a small canton and numerous stripes of blue, white and gold.[27]

In the 1620s and 1630s, striped ensigns gave way to ensigns with plain-coloured fields and the cross of St George in a canton. Red ensigns were made at Chatham in 1621 and later; and red ensigns, white ensigns and blue ensigns were listed in dockyard inventories at Deptford and Portsmouth in 1633, by which time striped ensigns were becoming obsolete in the navy. Some of these plain ensigns had coats of arms or badges, such as a rose and crown or an anchor, on them.[28]

Ensigns were now coming to be regarded as the primary flag of nationality. Captain Nathaniel Boteler, whose *Dialogues* were mainly written in the 1630s, says of ensigns:

They are placed in the sterns or poops of ships; and few ships there are, whether men-of-war or merchantmen, that are without them.

And their service is, that when any strange ships meet one with another at sea, or find one another in any harbour or road, by the showing abroad these Ensigns or Colours, it is known to one another of what country they are and to what place they belong.

Boteler's discussion of flags is printed in Appendix B.

Fleet tactics were still experimental in the navy of Charles I, and flag arrangements varied, but large fleets of warships were sometimes divided into three squadrons: the centre, commanded by the Admiral of the Fleet; the van by the vice admiral; and the rear by the rear admiral; each squadron with a vice admiral and a rear admiral of its own. In October 1625 the three squadrons of a fleet sent against Cadiz were assigned squadron colours – red for the admiral's squadron, blue for the vice admiral's and white for the rear admiral's. The commander-in-chief, Sir Edward Cecil, was allowed to fly the Standard at the main; the vice and rear admirals of his squadron flew red ensigns (that is, red flags with a canton of St George's cross) at the fore and mizzen mastheads respectively. The admiral, vice admiral and rear admiral of the blue squadron flew plain blue flags at the appropriate masthead, and the flag officers of the white squadron flew white flags in the same way. The other ships in the fleet were distinguished by pennants; red at the main for the admiral's squadron, blue at the fore for the vice admiral's, and white at the mizzen for the rear admiral's.[29]

The type of pennant that was becoming standard was smaller than the decorative streamers of the 16th century, usually slit into two tails at the fly, and had St George's cross at the hoist. Boteler says of pennants:

The use of them is to distinguish the Squadrons of great fleets by hanging them out in the tops of such ships as carry no flags . . . But besides this use, in great ships and especially such as belong to the King, they are often used by way of trim and bravery; and are then hung out at every yard arm and at the heads of the masts.

The second half of the 17th century is a period particularly rich in documentation of the flags used in the British navy. The fleet actions of the three Anglo-Dutch wars of 1652-4, 1665-7, and 1672-4 are recorded in unprecedented detail by the drawings of the Elder Willem Van de Velde (1610-93), who was present at the battle of Scheveningen in 1653 and some of the subsequent actions. His work and that of his son Willem the Younger (1633-1707) set a new standard of technical accuracy in marine art; they are the fountainhead of the English tradition of specialist marine art.[30] The written records available to the flag historian improve dramatically after the Restoration chiefly because of the great mass of information accumulated by Samuel Pepys in his career as naval administrator and reformer under Charles II and James II, much of it now to be found in the Pepys Manuscripts at Magdalene College, Cambridge.[31]

The eleven years between the execution of Charles I in 1649 and the restoration of the monarchy in 1660 were a period of special sensitivity to political symbols, and flag designs were altered several times to reflect political changes. In 1649, the Government abolished the Royal Standard. The union of England and Scotland had been a union of crowns only, so that its symbol, the Union Flag, disappeared as well. The first idea[32] was to restore the flag of St George for all purposes at sea, but this was soon superseded by a range of flags based on the cross of St George impaling the Irish harp. The commonest form was the jack, in which the cross and harp occupied the whole flag (Plate II, no. 13): a larger version of this was used as an admiral's flag.[33] Another pattern of command flag had the cross and harp in two shields in a yellow oval panel on a red field (Figs. 13, 14).[34] A 'standard, apparently made for use by the Generals at Sea, the supreme officers of the Commonwealth navy, had the cross and harp within a wreath on a red flag: an example of this pattern, preserved for many years in Chatham Dockyard, is now in the National Maritime Museum (Plate XI).[35]

The cross of St George, red on a white ground, continued in use in the canton of ensigns and at the hoist of pennants. During the First Dutch War the system of dividing fleets into squadrons by colour was further developed, and all the ships in a fleet began systematically to use ensigns, as well as pennants, of the squadron colour. In 1653 the seniority of the colours was altered from red, blue, white, to red, white, blue. The only flag common to all the ships in the fleet was the cross and harp jack.[36]

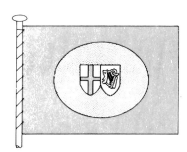

13 Pattern of English command flag used during the First Dutch War (1652-4)

The fluctuating political situation in 1658-60 was reflected in a series of rapid changes in flags. In 1658 Cromwell's standard as Lord Protector, in which the cross of St George was quartered with the cross of St Andrew and the Irish Harp, and surmounted by an escutcheon with Cromwell's personal coat of arms (Fig. 15), became the 'Standard for the General of his Highnesse fleet' and the Cross and Harp jack was replaced by the old Union Jack with the addition of a harp in the centre (Plate II, no. 14).[37] The death of Oliver Cromwell in September 1658 and the removal from power of his son in May 1659 resulted in further alterations in national heraldry but it is not known how far this affected sea flags before the Restoration of the monarchy the following May.

14 'The Battle of Scheveningen, 1653', grisaille by the Elder Van de Velde (detail)

15 Personal 'standard' of Oliver Cromwell

On the return of Charles II, the flags of the Commonwealth were replaced by the flags that had been in use before 1649. On 13 May the 24-year-old Samuel Pepys, then secretary to Edward Mountagu, one of the Generals at Sea, was on board the *Naseby*, the flagship of the fleet that was sailing over to Holland to fetch Charles II. New Royalist flags had been ordered but had not arrived in time and Pepys's *Diary* contains a description of the hurried preparation of makeshifts:

Then to the Quarter Deck, upon which the taylors and painters were at work cutting out of some pieces of yellow cloth into the

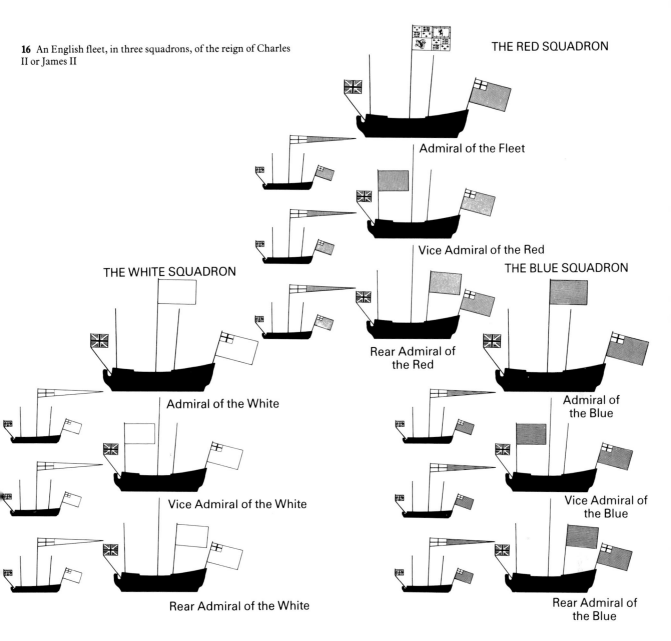

16 An English fleet, in three squadrons, of the reign of Charles II or James II

THE RED SQUADRON

Admiral of the Fleet

Vice Admiral of the Red

THE WHITE SQUADRON

Rear Admiral of the Red

THE BLUE SQUADRON

Admiral of the White

Vice Admiral of the White

Rear Admiral of the White

Admiral of the Blue

Vice Admiral of the Blue

Rear Admiral of the Blue

fashion of a crown and CR and put it upon a fine sheet, and that into the flag instead of the State's arms; which, after dinner, was finished and set up . . . In the afternoon a council of war, only to acquaint them that the Harp must be taken out of all their flags, it being very offensive to the King.

Within a few days the *Naseby* was resplendently decked in silk flags for the King.[38]

The arrangement of large fleets of warships now settled into a pattern (Fig. 16) that formed the theoretical basis of squadronal organization for the next two hundred years, although it was frequently modified in response to local conditions. A fleet consisted of three squadrons – red, white and blue. The Admiral of the Fleet (the admiral of the red squadron) flew the Union flag at the main, unless he was the Lord High Admiral and flew the Royal Standard; the vice and rear admirals of his squadron flew red flags at the fore and mizzen respectively. The admiral of the white squadron flew a plain white flag at the main, and his vice and rear admirals flew it respectively at the fore and mizzen. Similarly, the three flag officers of the blue squadron flew blue flags at main, fore and mizzen respectively. The private ships, but not the admirals, flew long pennants with

21

17 An episode in the Battle of Solebay 1672 (from a set of drawings, attributed to T. Phillips, in the Dartmouth Collection)

St George's cross at the hoist, and the fly either of the squadronal colour, or else striped lengthwise, red, white and blue – the 'common' or 'union' pennant, which was introduced in 1661 (Plate III, no. 23). Pennants were as a rule flown at the main.[39] Every ship in the fleet had ensigns of the squadronal colour at the ensign staff, and Union Jacks at the jack staff. This 'classic' arrangement was seen in its fullest development in the fleet actions of the Second and Third Dutch Wars. Ships that were not attached to a fleet or under the command of a flag officer wore colours as if they were part of the red squadron – red ensign, jack, and a red or tricolour pennant.

Throughout the 17th century the Royal Standard at the main, as well as indicating the presence of the king, was used by the Lord High Admiral. Occasionally, before 1649, the right to hoist the Royal Standard was granted to a fleet admiral who was not Lord High Admiral, and this was a coveted privilege. After the Restoration, the right to wear the Standard was more strictly controlled, and in 1702 it was definitively restricted to ships which actually had the sovereign on board. Other members of the Royal Family had (and still have) banners of their own which could be used on board ship (Plate XII).

The design of the anchor and cable flag traditionally known as the Admiralty Flag but properly the flag of the Lord High Admiral (Plate I, no. 9), originated early in the 17th century as a badge for the Lord High Admiral; a number of variations on the anchor and cable theme are recorded in flags and seals before 1649.[40] At the Restoration the horizontally placed yellow anchor and cable on a red field was accepted as the distinguishing flag of the Lord High Admiral, but it was rarely used as a command flag in ships of war because the Lord High Admiral used the Royal Standard instead, unless the king himself was present. After 1702, when the Royal Standard was restricted to the sovereign, the anchor flag was used by the Lord High Admiral or (since the office was for most of the time in commission) by a ship carrying two or more members of the Board of Admiralty. In 1964 the Board was dissolved and the anchor flag is now, like the Standard, the prerogative of the sovereign (who is her own Lord High Admiral).

The principal use of the anchor flag at sea since the reign of Charles II has been as one of a triad of flags – Royal Standard at the main, anchor flag at the fore, Union at the mizzen – which came to be used when the sovereign was on board a Royal Navy ship. The roots of this custom go back to the Restoration. The diarist Edward Barlow, who was on board the *Naseby* in May 1660 when she was waiting off the Dutch coast to bring Charles II back to England, recorded that: 'all things were ready for his acceptance, and all the ships being made as fine as possibly they could, our ship having flying three silk flags, one being the standard of England, and another having the anchor and cable in it, belonging to the Duke of York, and the other all red, with sixteen silk pennants or streamers (and a silk jack and a silk ancient) with nine streamers of another sort; and having a cloth of scarlet going round about her, and all her round tops wound about with the same, the ship being as clean washed and scraped as a trencher.'[41] Among the earliest pieces of evidence for the use of the Standard, anchor flag and Union together is a painting by Willem Van de Velde the Younger of the *Royal Prince* in 1672 with Charles II and James, Duke of York (later King James II), on board (see front cover).[42] The three flags are still used when the Queen is aboard one of her ships. The same combination of flags was also used in the 18th and 19th centuries at the launching of a naval ship (Fig. 18)

and sometimes on other occasions of celebration. In October 1750, for instance, HMS *Centurion* was in Tunis Bay and the ship's logs note: 'Being his Majesty's Birth Day hoisted the Anchor and Hope, Standard and Union at the Fore Main & Miz'n Topmast heads, & fired 21 guns.'[43]

The flags used by James, Duke of York, form a story in themselves. From 1660 to 1673 he was Lord High Admiral and flew the Royal Standard or the anchor flag at the main. As commander-in-chief at the Battle of Lowestoft in 1665 James flew the Royal Standard and Prince Rupert, Admiral of the White Squadron and second in command, flew the Union at the main. When James was deprived by the Test

18 'HMS *Buckingham* at her launch in 1751', oil painting by John Cleveley the Elder

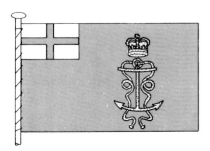

19 Personal ensign of King James II

Acts of 1673 of the post of Lord High Admiral, he used instead a flag and ensign with the device of the Admiral of Scotland, a horizontal blue anchor on a white field. When he succeeded to the throne in 1685 he was again Lord High Admiral of England and used a special flag in which the anchor was placed vertically and surmounted by a crown, and a red ensign with the same badge in the fly (Fig. 19).[44] These flags did not outlast James's removal from the throne in the 'Glorious Revolution' of 1688-9. On his

20 'Protestant standard' of William of Orange (King William III), 1688-9, with his arms impaled with his wife's; from Allard (Bibl. A 9)

voyage to take over the crown, William III apparently used a Standard with the words FOR THE PROTESTANT RELIGION AND THE LIBERTIES OF ENGLAND (Fig. 20).[45]

The pattern of the Union Flag and Jack generally adopted in the late 17th century and until 1801 was the pattern ordained in 1606. There is, however, tantalizing evidence of experiments in the 1660s with a version of the flag that foreshadowed the modern pattern by including a red saltire to represent Ireland within the white saltire of Scotland. The drawing in Figure 21 by the Elder Van de Velde of the *Henry* was made around 1661: it is one of a number of drawings and paintings that show such a design, but no documentary evidence about such a flag has yet been unearthed.[46]

In the Restoration navy the officers of a fleet held office by appointment only, not by rank: that is, they were appointed not to the permanent rank of, say, vice admiral, but to the temporary appointment of vice admiral of the blue squadron; after the fleet in question had finished its appointed task, the officer ceased to be a vice admiral, and he could not fly a flag in his own right. Commanders of expeditions were often given permission to fly special flags: for example, officers commanding squadrons in the Mediterranean or West Indies were regularly authorized to fly a Union Flag at the main as long as they were outside home waters.[47] There were also special pennants for officers not authorised to fly a full flag: a red pennant with St George's cross at the hoist but broader than the ordinary warship pennant (Fig. 22), was allotted in 1674 to the officer commanding in the Downs (off the east coast of Kent); and a

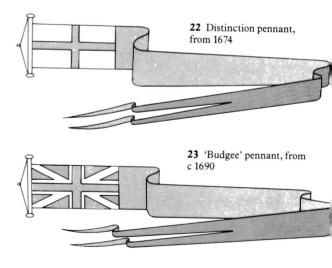

22 Distinction pennant, from 1674

23 'Budgee' pennant, from c 1690

21 The *Henry*, c 1661; drawing by the Elder Van de Velde (detail)

pennant called the 'Budgee pennant', a red broad pennant with the Union at the hoist (Fig. 23) was used in the 1690s by officers commanding outside home waters. Out of these special pennants developed the plain red and blue broad pennants used by commodores – a title which dates in the Royal Navy from about 1690 – seen in paintings of 18th-century actions.[48]

After the Third Dutch War the Royal Navy stopped fighting the Dutch and at the end of the century the main enemy was the French. The plain white admiral's flag and the white ensign were easily confused with the white flags used by the French navy; accordingly, in 1702, the white flag of flag officers of the white squadron was replaced by a flag of St George, and the white ensign was given a broad cross of St George throughout.[49] In 1707, following the Act of Union, the Union replaced the cross of St George in the canton of the ensigns, though not in the masthead pennants. In 18th-century ensigns the union in the canton tended to occupy a quarter of the area of the ensign, or a little less, in contrast to the earlier ensigns with St George's cross, in which the canton was generally a good deal smaller. Between 1707 and 1801 there was no important change in the design of the main command flags and colours of the British navy. Some of the regulations on the use of flags in the navy were laid down in the *Regulations and Instructions Relating to His Majesty's Service at Sea*: the section 'Of Colours' from the first edition (1731) is printed in Appendix D.

The colours of an 18th-century British warship (Fig. 24) were thus: the ensign, of the squadronal colour, or red if an independent command; the jack, which, following changes in rig around the 1720s, ceased to be worn at sea and since then has generally been hoisted only in harbour; and the pennant, sometimes with its fly of the colour of the ensign, otherwise striped lengthwise red, white and blue.[50] Since the 1720s the pennant has been the permanent distinguishing mark of a warship, kept flying all the time unless struck on the hoisting of a command flag or a broad pennant. It has never been obligatory to wear an ensign all the time at sea.

24 'A naval brigantine sloop, 1752', oil painting by John Cleveley the Elder

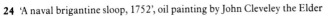

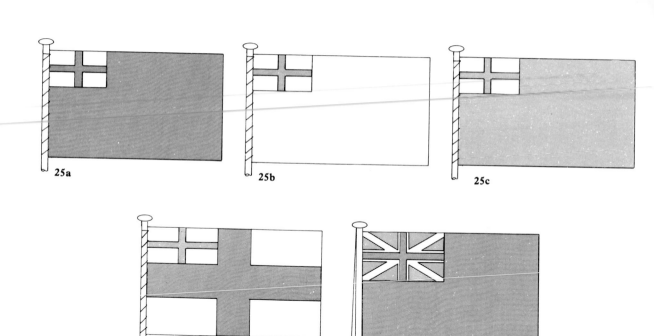

25a   25b   25c

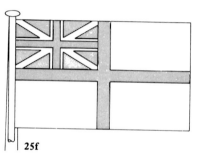 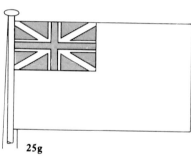

25d   25e

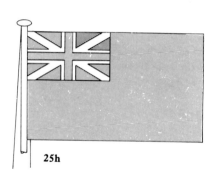

25f   25g   25h

25 The development of British naval ensigns:

a: Red ensign c 1620-1707
b: White ensign c 1630-1702
c: Blue ensign c 1630-1707
d: White ensign 1702-7
e: Red ensign 1707-1800
f: White ensign 1707-1800

g: Alternative white ensign (for use in home waters), 1707-c 1720
h: Blue ensign 1707-1800
i: Red ensign 1801-64 (British merchant ensign from 1864)
j: White ensign 1801-
k: Blue ensign 1801-64 (Royal Naval Reserve ensign from 1864)

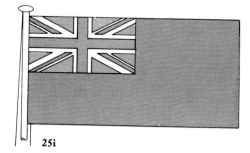

25i

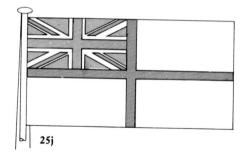 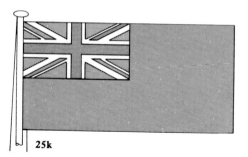

25j   25k

26 'The Battle of the Saints 1782', oil painting by Thomas Mitchell (detail). See p. 28

In addition to the pennant, warships often flew vanes at empty mastheads. These were short, blunt pennants, sometimes on a rigid framework, which were used by merchant ships as well as warships. The vanes of warships were generally of the squadronal colour, though some late-18th-century fleets were equipped with sets of different vanes in more than one colour which were used to distinguish individual ships.[51]

As the Royal Navy's responsibilities in defending and extending a world-wide empire grew in the 18th century, the 17th-century organization into a single enormous fleet with nine flag officers commanding nine squadrons was abandoned. Instead of being appointed to a temporary job in a particular fleet, officers obtained permanent tenure of rank and, once appointed to a flag, gained promotion by moving up the list as those above them died off. Up to 1743, the total number of active flag officers at any time was limited to nine; after that year the restriction was lifted, so that several admirals, vice admirals and rear admirals of each colour could exist, and the number of flag officers grew rapidly. The ladder of promotion incorporated squadronal colours: a man would normally receive his flag as rear admiral of the blue and advance through rear admiral of the white, rear admiral of the red, vice admiral of the blue, vice admiral of the white, vice admiral of the red, admiral of the blue and admiral of the white, until finally, if he lived long enough, he reached the rank of Admiral of the Fleet. While a rear admiral he flew his flag at the mizzen; while a vice admiral, at the fore; and when he became a full admiral, at the main. The Admiral of the Fleet flew the Union at the main. The system was extremely inflexible in that it was impossible to overtake those above you on the list; but this did not stop the Admiralty appointing a man from well down the list to command a squadron or a fleet if he was felt to be 'the best man for the job'; however, no flag officer could be placed under the orders of someone below him on the list. Thus there came about a reversal of the 17th-century arrangement: instead of taking his colour from the squadron he was appointed to, a flag officer had a rank and colour in his own right, and the ships under his command took their colour from him. A large fleet might have numerous flag officers (though never as many as the great fleets of the 17th century), a smaller one only one: at the Battle of the 'Glorious First of June' in 1794, Lord Howe's fleet had six flagships besides his own; at the battle of the Nile (1798) Nelson, a rear admiral of the blue, was the only flag officer present.

The theoretical principle – that a flag officer flew a

flag of his own colour at the appropriate masthead, and the ships under his command took their ensign colour from his flag – was often inconvenient in practice, and was repeatedly modified by special order in the naval engagements of the second half of the 18th century and later. If there were two flag officers of the same colour in a fleet, a vice admiral of the blue and a rear admiral of the blue for instance, and the commander-in-chief felt it was useful to differentiate ships under their command, the ships in one squadron might be ordered to wear ensigns of a different colour. Alternatively, if the commander-in-chief had no tactical use for distinguishing the ships of the fleet by colour, he might order all ships to wear ensigns of the same colour. This was often done when there was any danger of one of the squadronal colours being confused with the ensigns of an enemy. In 1782, when the Royal Navy was fighting the French, who used white colours, both Rodney and Howe issued orders to their fleets that all ships wear red ensigns in action; so Rodney's fleet at the Battle of the Saints (Fig. 26) that year fought under red ensigns, although he was an admiral of the white and flew a flag of St George at the main.[52] When in 1794 the French adopted the tricolour, the white ensign became more easily distinguishable: at the Battle of the Nile in 1798, Nelson, as Rear Admiral of the Blue, had his blue flag at the mizzen, but all the British ships hoisted white ensigns.[53]

In the last quarter of the 18th century a change in rigging affected the wearing of ensigns, which had up to then been worn on an ensign staff at the stern. A new sail, known as the 'spanker' had a boom at its foot which projected over the stern rail of the ship, and the ensign staff was in the way. Accordingly ensigns at sea came to be hoisted from the peak of the gaff, although ensign staffs went on being used on some ships where the spanker was not rigged. With the demise of the sailing warship after the middle of the 19th century, the ensign staff began to come back into use. Current Royal Navy practice is that the ensign is placed on an ensign staff when a ship is at anchor and transferred to a halyard on the super-structure when she gets under way.[54]

On 1 January 1801, the United Kingdom of Great Britain and Ireland came into existence and Ireland came to be represented in the Union and the ensigns. The emblem chosen to represent Ireland was the so-called 'cross of St Patrick', a red saltire on a white field. This emblem, originating in the arms of the

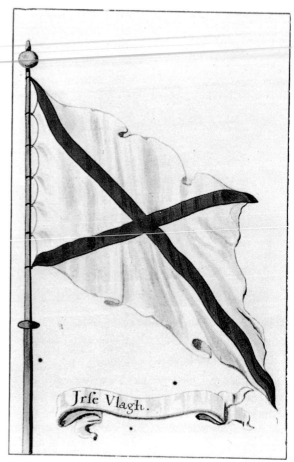

27 Irish red saltire flag, from the flag book of Paulus Van der Dussen c 1690 (Bibl. A 8)

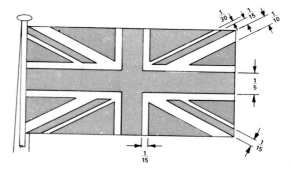

28 Modern proportions, Royal Navy Pattern Union Flag and Jack. Fractions are in relation to the hoist or breadth

29 (left) 'HMS Victory at Trafalgar', oil painting by J.M.W. Turner, 1824 (detail); at the damaged foremast is Nelson's flag as Vice Admiral of the White

28

30 HMS *Raleigh*, lithography by T.G. Dutton, 1850; at the main is the broad pennant of a commodore second class

Anglo-Irish family of Fitzgerald, had been occasionally used as an emblem of Ireland in the 17th century and appears in several late 17th and 18th century flag books (Fig. 27).[55] In 1783 the red saltire was adopted as the badge of the new Order of St Patrick. The arrangement of the crosses in the Union of 1801 was, in the technical description of the heralds: 'Azure, the crosses saltires of Saint Andrew and Saint Patrick, quarterly per saltire counterchanged argent and gules; the latter fimbriated of the second, surmounted by the cross of Saint George of the third fimbriated as the saltire'. The counterchanging, the device by which the red saltire is below the white in the hoist and above it in the fly, was designed to make the saltires more equal in status; if the red saltire were centred in the white, the cross of St Andrew would appear as a mere white border to the red cross of St Patrick; this would probably have upset sensibilities in Scotland even more than the Union of 1606 had. The design chosen, by putting the Scottish saltire uppermost in the first quarter (the upper hoist quarter), gives a slight precedence to Scotland; to fly the flag upside-down reverses the precedence. There have at various times since 1801 been minor variants

of the design: Figure 28 shows the current Royal Navy pattern.[56]

The new design was immediately introduced into the red, white, and blue ensigns, which thus assumed the modern form.

The Royal Standard was also altered in 1801 and after four and a half centuries the claim of the English kings to the throne of France which the presence of the fleurs-de-lis in the Standard had represented was implicitly abandoned. The arms of the Electorate of Hanover were placed in an escutcheon which was surmounted by the 'electoral bonnet' of Hanover (Plate I, no.6); from 1816, this was altered to a crown, the electorate having become a kingdom (Plate I, no.7). On the accession of Queen Victoria to the English throne, the two crowns were separated; the Hanoverian escutcheon was removed and the royal arms assumed their modern form (Plate I, no. 8).[57]

At the Battle of Trafalgar, the English flag officers were: Horatio, Viscount Nelson, Vice Admiral of the White, flying St George's cross at the fore of the *Victory*; Cuthbert Collingwood, Vice Admiral of the Blue, with a blue flag at the fore in the *Royal*

Sovereign; and William Carnegie, Earl of Northesk, Rear Admiral of the White, with the cross of St George at the mizzen in the *Britannia*. All the ships in the fleet wore white ensigns in accordance with an order issued by Nelson on 10 October 1805: 'When in presence of an Enemy, all the ships under my command are to bear White Colours and a Union Jack is to be suspended from the fore-topgallant stay'.[58] The *Victory* seems to have had her ensign at the peak, but some of the ships in the fleet wore their ensigns at ensign staffs.

In November 1805, by way of tribute to the navy's victories, a rank of Admiral of the Red, flying a red flag at the main, was created. The decree spoke of 'restoring' the rank, but in fact it was quite new. Previously the rank above Admiral of the White had been Admiral of the Fleet, flying the Union at the main.

The following year, for the first time, regulations were made for the rank of commodore, which had had only a somewhat murky legal status for most of the 18th century. The regulations issued in 1806 included provision for a 'temporary rank of Commodore, which shall be distinguished by a Broad Pendant, Red, White or Blue ... If the Commodore commands the ship himself the Pendant shall have a large white ball near the staff'. The regulations of 1826 divided commodores into first class (when they had a captain commanding the ship

under them) and second class (when they command the ship themselves): commodores of the first class were to use a red broad pennant, or white broad pennant with a red cross of St George through it; commodores of the second class a blue broad pennant.[59]

By the 19th century, the tactical division of fleets into three squadrons was more or less obsolete, and the decision by Nelson and others to order their fleets to wear ensigns of a single colour demonstrates that the distinction of ships by squadronal colour had ceased to be useful. Finally in 1864 the whole system was abolished. By an order of 9 July 1864 (App. E) the Royal Navy abandoned the use of the red and the blue ensigns and pennants (the tricolour pennant had been discontinued some years before) and adopted white ensigns, masthead pennants, command flags, and broad pennants. The blue ensign, with an appropriate badge in the fly, was allocated to ships in public service and in the non-military departments of the navy; in 1866 the use of defaced blue ensigns was extended to ships in the service of the colonies. The plain blue ensign was to be worn by merchant ships 'commanded by Officers of the Royal Naval Reserve Force and fulfilling in other respects the conditions required to entitle them to the privilege'. Red ensigns were to continue to be the normal colours of the merchant service and other privately owned British ships.[60]

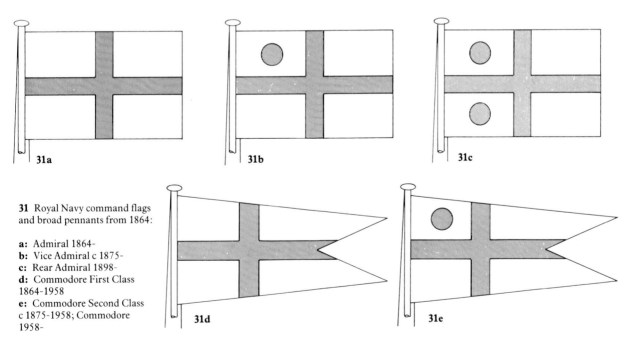

31a   31b   31c

31 Royal Navy command flags and broad pennants from 1864:

a: Admiral 1864–
b: Vice Admiral c 1875–
c: Rear Admiral 1898–
d: Commodore First Class 1864-1958
e: Commodore Second Class c 1875-1958; Commodore 1958–

31d   31e

By the 1870s, steamships had become common in the navy and it could no longer be assumed that all flagships would always have three distinct mastheads. Since the beginning of the 18th century a system had existed for differentiating the flags of admirals, vice admirals and rear admirals in boats without masts by adding balls to the flags of the junior flag officers. As Royal Navy flagships ceased necessarily to have three masts it became usual to include a small red ball in the upper hoist quarter of the flags of vice admirals and the broad pennants of commodore second class, and two red balls in the flags of rear admirals. At first the balls in the flags of rear admirals were both in the upper hoist quarter; in 1898, when the system was regularized, the balls were enlarged and one was placed in the upper, the other in the lower hoist quarter.[61]

This development produced the main series of colours and flags of command which have remained in use in the navy to the present day, with the exception that the rank of commodore first class was placed in abeyance in 1958: the modern commodore flies a broad pennant with a red ball (Fig. 31e).

The flags used by Royal Navy ships in the battles of the First World War are a special episode. It was (and still is) normal in action to wear at least two ensigns, in case one was shot away. Since the German Imperial naval ensign (Plate XVI, no. 29) was in poor visibility liable to confusion with the white ensign, the Admiralty issued a succession of orders to the navy about the use of additional flags. On 2 September 1914, an order went out that ships hoist a blue as well as a white ensign when going into action or approaching a suspicious vessel. Four days later this was revoked and it was ordered that a Union Flag be used in addition to the white ensign. From November 1914 to the beginning of 1916 a red ensign was to be the additional battle flag. Finally, on 11 January 1916, the Union was re-introduced and remained in use for the rest of the war. The ships that fought at Jutland thus had, like the fleet at Trafalgar, white ensigns and an extra Union.[62]

The flags used by the Royal Navy today are illustrated in the official book *Flags of All Nations*, and detailed instructions on their use are contained in the current *Queen's Regulations for the Royal Navy*. Useful summaries are in Volume I of the *Admiralty Manual of Seamanship* and in *Flags of the World*, of which the 1981 edition was edited by Captain E.M.C. Barraclough and W.G. Crampton.

32 'The Royal Yacht *Britannia* at Greenwich, 1954', oil painting by Normal Wilkinson (detail); compare the flag combination on the *Royal Prince* in 1672 (front cover)

CHAPTER 2

Flags of British ships other than the Royal Navy

Colours of merchant ships

The history of the colours used by British merchant ships is less well recorded than the history of naval flags. The administrative machine that ran the Royal Navy generated a mass of documentation on its flags; there is nothing equivalent for the 'merchant navy'. The main official concern with merchant ship flags since the 17th century has been to prevent unauthorized use of flags reserved for the navy.

In the 16th century merchant ships were less flamboyant in flag display than were the king's ships. Although privately owned ships no doubt put out extra flags and streamers for special occasions, under normal circumstances Tudor merchant ships flew nothing more elaborate than small, rather square flags of St George's cross, at one or more mastheads.

In the 14th century privately owned ships had been in the habit of using the Royal Standard as a national flag, but by Tudor times this was only flown with special permission and on voyages with royal support. In 1495 John Cabot was authorized to use the royal arms on his expedition to North America. A century later, in 1595, Drake and Hawkins took flags with the royal arms and streamers with the royal badges, as well as flags of St George, on the voyage to the West Indies on which they both died.[63]

At the beginning of the 17th century some merchant ships were using striped ensigns similar to those worn by the king's ships. The proclamation of 1606 laid down that all privately owned ships fly the Union at the main and St George's cross (or St Andrew's) at the fore. These remained the 'correct' flags until 1634, when the proclamation restricting the Union to the king's ships again made the cross of St George the official national flag for English merchantmen. At about the same time the red ensign, with St George's cross in the canton, was coming into general use. In 1674 a proclamation reaffirming the ban on merchant ships using the 'king's jack' stipulated that they should fly 'those usually heretofore worn on Merchants Ships, viz.

The Flag and Jack White, with a Red Cross, (commonly called, Saint George's Cross) passing quite through the same; And the Ensign Red, with the like Cross in a Canton White, at the upper Corner thereof next to the staff'. Scottish merchant ships sometimes used an ensign with the cross of St Andrew in the canton (Plate II, no. 18).

The Proclamation of 1634 banning the use of the Union Flag and Jack by merchantmen did not settle the issue. Merchantmen continued to use the forbidden flag without authority and after the Restoration a series of orders were issued in an attempt to stamp the practice out. It was an issue that much perplexed the tidy mind of Samuel Pepys and his papers contain detailed notes on the issue including various reasons why merchant captains wanted to use the Jack; it carried exemption from port dues in France and from the requirement to take a pilot in Holland; it exacted the 'Right of the Flag'; and it gave protection against 'having their men pressed from them by greater ships or being otherwise obstructed or denied reasonable aids and favours from all hands as being in the King's service'. Pepys also wanted to stop 'Rogues putting up the Jack and by virtue thereof going away with smuggled goods'.[64] Orders attempting to enforce the ban were issued in 1661 and 1666; the proclamation of 1674 included a ban on 'Jacks in Shape and mixture of Colours, so little different from those of His Majesty, as not to be without difficulty distinguished therefrom'. Further proclamations were issued in 1694 and 1702; that of 1694, which included a ban on 'any kind of Pendant whatsoever' and laid down special jacks for privateers and ships in the service of public departments, is printed as Appendix C. In 1707 the same warnings were included in the proclamation which established the new form of the ensign, with the Union instead of St George's cross in the canton.

The proclamations up to and including the one of 1702 permit the 'flag and jack' with St George's cross. In 1702, however, the admirals' flags of the flag

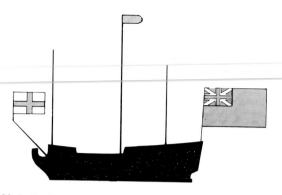

33 An English 18th-century merchant ship, with red ensign and St George's jack

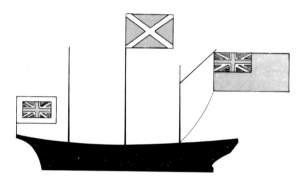

34 An English mid-19th century ship, with red ensign, company house flag, and white-bordered jack

know what legal justification, if any, there may have been for this. A note in the 1819 edition of Norie's *Maritime Flags of All Nations* reads:

The red Ensign is the only one allowed to be hoisted on board of Merchant Ships; but in case the said Ensign be much torn, and is being repaired, or a ship be at sea, without having one on-board, then a blue, or St George's [ie. white] Ensign may be hoisted, provided it has a red border of the following width, at the top, bottom, and fly end. For 800 tons and upward, not less than 14 inches border. All ships under 800 tons burthen, 9 inches border.

From the middle of the 19th century it became customary for British merchant ships to use as a jack a version of the Union Jack with a white border all round it (Fig. 36).[66] This flag was introduced in 1823 as a signal for calling a pilot in Marryat's *Code of Signals for the Merchant Service* and later came to be worn as a jack. It is still a legally permitted jack for merchant ships.

The 1864 re-organization of naval flags did not affect the position of the red ensign as the normal colours of a British merchant ship. It did, however, lay down that merchant ships could be granted an Admiralty warrant to wear a blue ensign if the captain and a proportion of the crew were members of the recently formed Royal Naval Reserve. The criteria for warrants to wear the blue ensign, which have been modified from time to time, are laid down in the *Queen's Regulations*. The current (1983) regulations for merchant ships are:

The officer commanding a ship other than a fishing vessel must be an officer on the Retired or Emergency Lists of the Royal Navy or a Commonwealth Navy, or an officer on the Active or Retired Lists of any branch of the Reserves of such navies. If the rank held on one of these Lists by the officer commanding the ship is below that of Commander, at least one other officer in the ship's company must be an officer on one of the Lists mentioned.[67]

Earlier this century when the regulations were that the commander had to be a Reserve officer and ten of the crew members of the Royal Naval Reserve, the blue ensign was often to be seen on prestigious liners. In 1912 the *Titanic* hoisted a blue ensign for her one and only voyage.

The law on the colours to be worn by British merchant ships is embodied in the 1894 *Merchant Shipping Act*:

The Red Ensign usually worn by merchant ships, without any defacement or modification whatsoever is hereby declared to be the proper national colours for all ships or boats belonging to any British subject, except in the case of Her Majesty's ships or boats,

officers of the white were altered and the flag of St George at a masthead became a naval command flag. Accordingly, by the time of the *Regulations* of 1731 (App. D) the use of the masthead flag of St George had been withdrawn from merchant ships and their proper colours were declared to be the red ensign and St George's jack. This jack remained part of the official colours of a British merchantman in the 18th century (Fig. 33), but marine paintings rarely show it, and it was probably little used.

Eighteenth-century merchantmen were forbidden to fly pennants, but instead often flew short vanes at the mastheads. Paintings of the period usually show these as being plain red.

Although the red ensign, in its successive forms, has been the normal legal ensign for British merchant ships since 1674, there is evidence, particularly during the first half of the 19th century, of merchant ships wearing white or blue ensigns.[65] It is hard to

This remains the current law, except that the powers formerly vested in the Admiralty were transferred in 1964 to the Secretary of State for Defence.

A common sight in British ports nowadays is a foreign merchant ship with a red ensign flying at the yard-arm. This is the so-called courtesy ensign: on leaving her home port it is customary for a ship to fly at the fore the merchant ensign of the country to which she is ultimately bound; and while in a foreign port she flies at the fore or yard-arm the ensign of the country being visited at the time.[68] This practice, though its roots are older, seems to have developed on the North Atlantic route in the 19th century. The *Great Western* and the *Sirius*, the first ships to make the crossing between Britain and America under steam, in 1838, are recorded to have flown the Stars

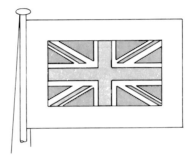

36 White bordered 'merchant jack' (*alias* 'pilot jack')

and Stripes at the fore. In 1845, when the *Great Britain* arrived in New York at the end of her maiden voyage, the *New York Herald* reporter noticed a bewildering array of flags:

From the heights she presented a grand and beautiful appearance. At every mast were colours streaming. At the gaff a large Union Flag of England flew gaily in the breeze. The first mast had the Austrian flag, the second the Russian, the third the Spanish, the fourth the French Tricolour, the main Union Jack and the foremast a blended flag of England and America, the Stars of this country blending with the blue, white and red of the Union of England and at the lower quartering the stripes.[69]

House flags of shipping companies

The use of special flags for the ships of a particular company can be traced back to the 16th century. In 1581 Queen Elizabeth granted to the Levant Company letters patent allowing them 'to set and place in the tops of their ships and other vessels the armes of England with the red crosse over the same, as heretofore they have used the red crosse'. This was a variant of the privilege sometimes granted to private

35 'An English merchant ship off Dover', oil painting by Charles Brooking (1723-59) (detail)

or in the case of any other ship or boat for the time being allowed to wear any other national colours in pursuance of a warrant from Her Majesty or from the Admiralty.

If any distinctive national colours, except such Red Ensign or except the Union Jack with a white border, or if any colours usually worn by Her Majesty's ships or resembling those of Her Majesty; or if the pennant usually carried by Her Majesty's ships or any pennant resembling that pennant are or is hoisted on board any ship or boat belonging to any British subject without warrant from her Majesty or from the Admiralty, the master of the ship or boat or the owner thereof, if on board the same, and every other person hoisting the colours or pennant, shall for each offence incur a fine not exceeding £500 . . .

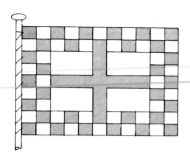

37 Jack of the Royal Africa Company ('Guinea Jack'), 17th-18th century

38 'The Guineaman *Madeross*, 1664', drawing by Edward Barlow, from his *Journal*

expeditions of wearing the Royal Standard, but amounted to a distinctive company flag.[70]

In the 17th century some of the great chartered trading companies used distinctive flags on their ships. The jack of the Royal Africa Company was a cross of St George within a double border of red and white chequers. Edward Barlow's drawing of the Guineaman *Madeross* (Fig. 38) in 1664 is an early illustration of the use of this flag. An actual example preserved in the Rijksmuseum, Amsterdam, is thought to have been captured in West Africa in 1665.[71] The flag appears regularly, sometimes in a rather garbled form, in flag plates of the late 17th and early 18th centuries. The last 'Guinea Company' was dissolved in 1752.

A more complex history is that of the various red and white striped flags of the Honourable East India Company (Fig. 39). The striped ensign with the cross of St George in the canton is first recorded shortly after the Restoration; the number of stripes

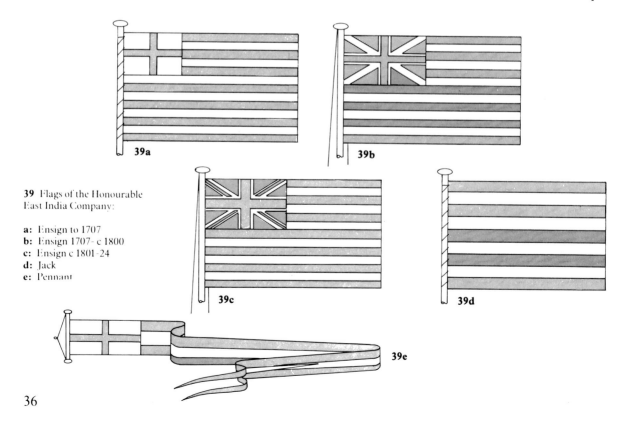

39 Flags of the Honourable East India Company:

a: Ensign to 1707
b: Ensign 1707- c 1800
c: Ensign c 1801-24
d: Jack
e: Pennant

39a

39b

39c

39d

39e

40 An East Indiaman (seen from two points of view), oil painting by Isaac Sailmaker (pre-1707)

varies in illustrations but thirteen is typical. In 1676, following the proclamation of 1674 stipulating the red ensign as the proper colours for English merchant ships, the ever-busy Pepys took issue with the continued use on the Company's ships of the striped ensign and it was accordingly agreed that they would only use the striped colours in Eastern waters and beyond St Helena in the Atlantic. Paintings of East Indiamen (Fig. 40) show that there existed a complete set of striped flags – ensign, jack, masthead flags and a pennant with St George at the hoist and the fly

striped red/white/red. The canton of the ensign changed with the red ensign: that is, the Union was incorporated in place of the cross of St George after 1707 and the Irish saltire was added after 1801. The striped ensign was abandoned by the Company's ships after 1824.[72]

The real origin of the modern British merchant shipping company house flag, however, seems to lie not in the flags of the chartered companies, but in the systems of 'private signals' for merchant ships that developed at the end of the 18th century. At Bidston

Hill, for instance, overlooking the Mersey opposite Liverpool, a signal station was erected in 1771 with a number of flagstaffs, each allotted to a particular shipowner; when a merchant ship approached the Mersey its impending arrival was signalled to Liverpool by hoisting its owner's special distinguishing flag. A number of Liverpool shipping company house flags are said to have originated in the flags used at Bidston Hill.[73]

The practice of flying the 'house flag' all the time seems to have become common after the end of the Napoleonic Wars. A probably apocryphal story is told of the origin of one of the oldest and most distinguished English house flags, that of the great Blackwall shipbuilding and shipowning firm of Wigram and Green. One of their ships, the *Sir Edward Paget*, off Spithead in 1824 with a flag of St George at the main, was ordered by the local admiral commanding to haul down the flag on the grounds that it was reserved to the Royal Navy as the flag of

41 Creamware jug, printed with the signal station at Bidston Hill, near Liverpool, dated 1788

42 *(below)* The Blackwaller *Alfred*, lithograph by T.G. Dutton 1847; she is making her number in Marryat's code, but in this lithograph the distinguishing pennant has been incorrectly coloured

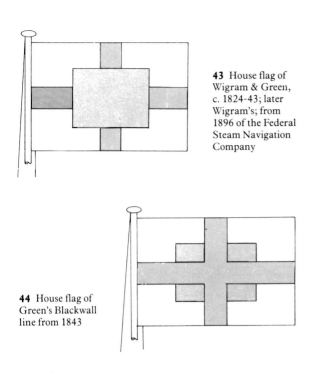

43 House flag of Wigram & Green, c. 1824-43; later Wigram's; from 1896 of the Federal Steam Navigation Company

44 House flag of Green's Blackwall line from 1843

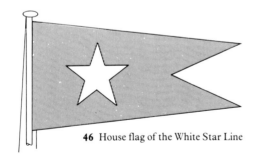

45 House flag of the Cunard Steamship Company

placed the rectangle under the cross (Fig. 44). Later the original flag became the house flag of the Federal Steam Navigation Company.

House flags are traditionally flown at the main, though one or two companies – notably Brocklebank's – have flown it at the fore instead. Occasionally a more complex arrangement is seen: when, in 1934, two of the great transatlantic liner companies, Cunard and White Star, merged, their ships for a time flew both house flags, one above the other; nowadays only the Cunard flag is used. House flags are also sometimes seen used as jacks at the bow.

A variant of the normal house flag is occasionally to be found used as a 'commodore's pennant'. These flags are used in place of the house flag by the commodore or senior master of a shipping company.[75]

House flags often appear in ship portraits of the 'clipper ship' age, having become more or less universal by the middle of the 19th century. House flags in paintings of this period can be elusive, and the problem is complicated by the fact that 19th-century shipping companies sometimes had different flags for the different ships of their fleets, so that if the ship's name is not known a good deal of research, and some luck, may be required before the flag is identified. In 1882 appeared the first edition of *Lloyd's Book of House Flags*; from this date there is a steady stream of books and charts of house flags and identifying a flag usually presents less of a problem. A selective list of sources on house flags is given in Section E of the Bibliography.

As well as by their house flags merchant steam ships are distinguished by funnel markings, which are sometimes related to the design of the house flag. The practice grew up in the early days of steam navigation. Funnel markings are usually recorded in the same books of reference as house flags.

Paintings of 19th- and 20th-century merchant ships sometimes show them flying large pennants with the ship's name written on them (Fig. 47). The use and design of name pennants are not standardized; they are a matter of personal taste.

Public service vessels

Before 1694 no distinction in flags was made between the navy's ships of war and vessels in the 'civil departments' of the navy or other branches of the king's service; the Union Jack was used by all ships

46 House flag of the White Star Line

an admiral of the white. To meet this objection a patch of blue cloth – a part of the chief officer's coat-tail in one version of the story – was stuck over the centre of the flag, and the red cross on white, with a blue rectangle over it (Fig. 43) was from that time the company house flag.[74] In 1843 the company split in two, Wigram's adopting the old flag while Green's

47 *Spinaway* (topsail schooner launched in 1877), watercolour by Reuben Chappell

'such as are of His Majesty's own or serve under His pay', as Boteler put it. In 1694 (App. C) it was laid down that vessels in these non-military branches of the king's service use a red jack with a Union in a rather large canton (which was the jack at the same time allocated to privateers) with the badge of the department in the fly. The designs of these badges were: for the Navy Board, a plain vertical anchor flanked by two smaller anchors; for the Transport Office a plain vertical anchor; for the Ordnance Board[76] a shield with three field guns and, on a chief, three cannon balls; and for the Victualling Office two anchors with cables crossed in saltire. Though the colours may have varied, these badges are still to be found in flag books of the first half of the 19th century (Fig. 48).

The placing of the badges varied. The regulations of 1731 (App. D) stated that the badge could be placed in the fly of the jack or the ensign; the regulations issued in 1806 laid down that it should be in the ensign. and those of 1844 stipulated that it

should be in both ensign and jack. Some 19th-century flag books show the badges in the centre of plain flags, which were used as masthead flags.

The new flag arrangements of 1864 changed the colour of the ensigns of public offices to blue. At first it was laid down that the jack should be the white-bordered Union (the 'merchant jack') but in 1868 this ruling was cancelled and a blue jack with the union in the canton and the badge in the fly was established. The design of this jack was similar to that of the ensign: the difference was, and is, that the jack is smaller than the ensign and sometimes square. The defaced blue ensign and jack are still the regulation colours for 'vessels employed in the service of any public office in the United Kingdom'; the badges are illustrated in the current edition of *Flags of all Nations*.[77]

The colours of 'revenue cutters' and other Customs and Excise vessels, which are also mentioned in the proclamation of 1694, were at first, the red ensign and jack with a 'castellated gateway'. An act of 1784

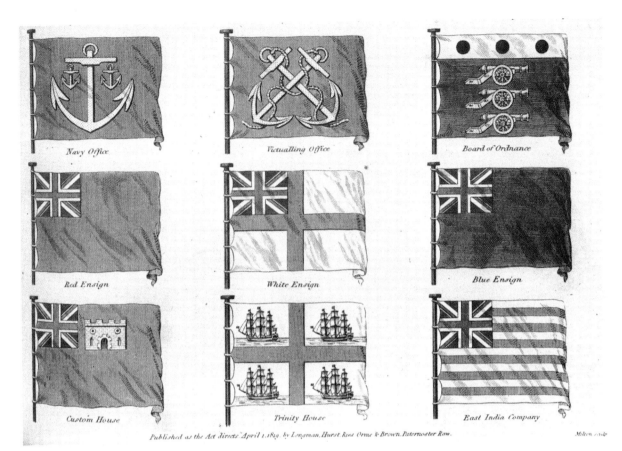

Navy Office

Victualling Office

Board of Ordnance

Red Ensign

White Ensign

Blue Ensign

Custom House

Trinity House

East India Company

48 Part of a flag plate from Rees's *Cyclopedia* (1820)

instructed Customs vessels to hoist a blue ensign and pennant, both with the castellated gateway, when giving chase. For a short period between 1815 and 1817 the Customs ensign was red with a yellow crown in the fly over an eight-pointed yellow star, with a red circle inside it containing the letters CH in yellow; together with a red pennant with the same device in the hoist. In the same period Excise vessels used a blue ensign and pennant with a white crown over a white star, inside which was EX in white in a blue circle. After 1817 Customs and Excise vessels again had only one ensign and pennant: the ensign red with a royal crown in the fly, the pennant red with the crown at the hoist. In 1872 Customs and Excise followed other public service flags and the colour of the field was altered to blue. These flags lasted till 1949, when a portcullis badge, reminiscent of the old 'castellated gateway', surmounted by a crown, was introduced.[78]

In November 1694 vessels in the service of the General Post Office were allocated the badge of 'a man on horseback blowing a Post horne'. This 'postboy' emblem is recorded in 19th century flag books and in paintings, both as a badge in a red ensign (Fig. 50) and by itself as a masthead flag.

From the end of the 17th to the middle of the 19th century the Post Office maintained a network of packet-boat services from various ports. These had some of the privileges of naval vessels: the

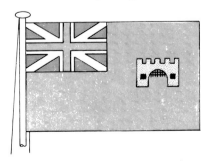

49 Customs ensign, in use from after 1707 until 1784

50 'Postboy' ensign, from the 1842 edition of Norie's *Maritime Flags* (Bibl. A28)

51 Royal Mail pennant, from *Flags of All Nations* (Bibl. B 9), 1889 edition

52 Royal Mail pennant, from *Flags of All Nations* (Bibl. B 9), 1916 edition

Regulations and Instructions Relating to His Majesty's Service at Sea issued in 1806 state that 'Packets employed by the post-office, and having Commanders appointed by Commission from the Admiralty, are permitted to carry a red ensign, a jack and a pendant.' About 1833 the colour of the ensign and pennant was changed from red to blue. Packets based at Falmouth, the main base for the Atlantic packet services, had individual flags for each vessel in the 1820s; these were flown at the fore.[79]

After 1839-40, when the award of a group of Admiralty mail contracts to Cunard and others launched the great Royal Mail steamship lines, the fate of the packets was sealed. The Falmouth service closed in 1850. In 1884 a special Royal Mail pennant, for ships carrying mails, was instituted. This bore a crown and the words ROYAL MAIL (Fig. 51); in 1902 a post-horn was added (Fig. 52).

53 Trinity House jack

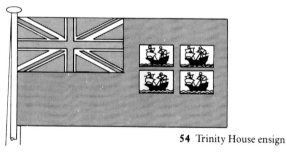

54 Trinity House ensign

Older than any of the flags of public bodies so far mentioned are those of the Corporation of Trinity House, a range of flags based on the arms granted to it in 1573 – the jack (Fig. 53), the ensign (Fig. 54), the burgee, and the flags of the Master and Deputy Master.[80]

Privateers

Privateers were 'private men of war', privately owned ships that carried 'letters of marque' licensing them to raid enemy commerce and take prizes. In the

55 A Trinity House cutter c 1810, detail from an oil painting by Thomas Whitcombe

reign of Elizabeth I, Drake and Hawkins, along with many others, were in effect privateers much of the time; their flags had much in common with those flown on the queen's own ships. In the 17th century, despite the proclamation of 1634, privateers often used the 'King's Jack', whether or not they had special warrant to do so, and tended to make themselves look like naval vessels. Official efforts to stop them were made from time to time, but ineffectively.[81]

The Proclamation of 1694 (App. C) introduced a

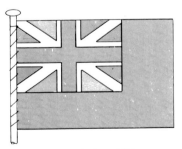

56 Privateer jack, from 1694

57 'The privateer *Fly*, 1779', oil painting by Francis Holman; she has the jack and pennant of a naval vessel

special 'privateer jack' (the so-called 'budgee jack') in which the Union appeared as rather a large canton in a red field (Fig. 56). This jack, together with the red ensign, remained the official colours of a British privateer until privateering was finally abolished in 1856. It appears, however, that 18th-century privateers continued to use both the Union Jack and the naval pennant. Eighteenth-century illustrations of privateers regularly show the Jack and pennant.

Yachts

The privilege now granted to numerous British yacht clubs to use ensigns other than the standard red ensign goes back to the earliest English yacht clubs. The yachts of the Cumberland Fleet (the ancestor of the Royal Thames Yacht Club), which was formed in 1775 for sailing on the Thames, used a version of the white ensign without the large cross of St George.[82] The members of the Yacht Club (which was formed at Cowes in 1815, became the Royal Yacht Club in 1820, and the Royal Yacht Squadron

in 1833) also used this version of the white ensign at first. The royal patronage of this club did not prevent the Admiralty taking steps in 1821 to enforce the ban on unauthorized use of the white ensign, and from 1821 to 1829 members could only use the ordinary red ensign. In 1829, however, the Admiralty issued a special warrant to the Royal Yacht Club for members' yachts to use the white ensign (the form with the large cross of St George). In the years following the same right was granted to certain other clubs, but in 1842 these additional warrants were

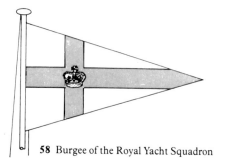

58 Burgee of the Royal Yacht Squadron

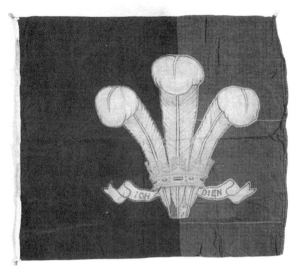

59 Flag used on the yacht *Britannia*, built in 1893 for the Prince of Wales (later King Edward VII). 99 × 117 cm

60 Bartholomew Roberts, from Captain Charles Johnson, *A General History of ... Pyrates*, 3rd ed., 1725

withdrawn and the use of the white ensign has been rigorously restricted ever since. Royal Yacht Squadron yachts are the only vessels outside the Royal Navy normally allowed to use the white ensign. A number of clubs have warrants for their members to use special defaced red or blue ensigns, or in some cases the plain blue ensign.[83]

The principal flags, apart from ensigns, used by British yachts are the burgee, the distinctive flag of the club, which is usually triangular in shape; and the personal flag of the owner, which is more often than not rectangular. Other flags flown by yachts are the flags or broad pennants of 'flag officers' of yacht clubs, private racing flags, and prize flags indicating races that have been won.[84]

Pirate flags

The few fragments of authentic information about the flags used by pirates in the 'golden age' of piracy in the 17th and 18th centuries tend to get lost in the

61 From *La Connoissance des Pavillons*, 1737 (Bibl. A 20)

flags bearing various symbols of death, for which the term 'Jolly Roger' came into use early in the 18th century. In 1717 an English ship was attacked to the west of Madeira by a French pirate 'wth Death's head in black in ye middle of a white Ensign', as one of those on board recorded.[85] In 1723 a number of pirates were hanged at Newport, Rhode Island, and the flag they had used was fixed to the gallows; this was 'a Black Flag with the Pourtrature of Death having an Hour-Glass in one Hand, and a Dart in the other, at the end of which was the Form of a Heart with three Drops of Blood, falling from it . . . This Flag they call'd Old Roger, and often us'd to say they would live and die under it'.[86] At about the same time another notorious pirate, Captain Bartholomew Roberts, is reported to have had a flag of his own reflecting a personal vendetta against Barbados and Martinique: 'The Jack had a man pourtray'd in it with a flaming Sword in his Hand, and standing on two Skulls subscribed ABH and AMH, i.e. a Barbadian's and a Martinican's Head' (Fig. 60).[87] A flag of rather the same type is given in early 18th-century flag books for the Barbary corsairs: it is red, with a winged hour-glass, an arm brandishing a sword, and a skull and cross-bones (Fig. 61).[88]

A 20th-century revival of the Jolly Roger tradition is the skull-and-crossbones flags used by British submarines in the First and Second World Wars and still in use in the Falkland Islands war of 1982. Extra symbols are sewn on to a submarine's 'Jolly Roger' flag to indicate its 'kills' or other exploits (Fig. 106).[89]

romantic image of the ubiquitous 'Jolly Roger'. Very often it must have suited pirates not to be recognized as such and they no doubt made much use of false colours to gain surprise. Some pirates used plain flags with a generally understood colour symbolism – black for death, or red (the 'bloody flag') for battle.

More individualistic and flamboyant were the

CHAPTER 3

Sea Flags of the United States of America

The early British settlers on the east coast of America used British flags on land and at sea, and British flags are the starting point in the story of North American flags. The first tangible evidence on the flags used by the colonists of British North America dates from 1630s, by which date the red ensign with a cross of St George in the canton was becoming accepted as the normal flag of English ships, and a similar flag was apparently in military use in Massachusetts as the 'King's Colours'. The dominant ideology of the colony was, however, a radical Puritanism that objected to even so basic a Christian symbol as the cross, as being a mark of sinful idolatry. In 1634 a local pastor named Roger Williams delivered a sermon in which he condemned the use of the cross in flags. Subsequently a move was made to remove the cross from the canton of the military colours at Salem and after a considerable row and a series of debates in the General Court, the change was confirmed and the Massachusetts militia adopted a red flag with a plain white canton (Fig. 62). It is likely, though not proven, that this curious crossless ensign was also used at sea. It lasted until the 1680s, when consciences had evidently become less tender and the cross was restored.[90]

The favourite symbol of New England in the late 17th and 18th centuries was a tree: oak, willow and pine trees appeared on the coinage of the Massachusetts Bay Colony between 1652 and 1682. Lieutenant Graydon's 1686 flag book illustrates as the flag of New England a flag of St George's cross with what appears to be an oak tree in the first quarter. Some other flag books illustrate a red ensign with, in the canton, a cross of St George with a tree in the first quarter (Fig. 63). It is likely that these two flags were both used by New England ships, respectively as a jack and an ensign, just as the St George's jack and the red ensign were used by English ships.[91] The tree was a long-lasting symbol: flags with a pine tree and the motto AN APPEAL TO HEAVEN were in use afloat at the beginning of the American Revolution in 1775, and later.[92]

The only officially authorized special flag for colonial ships of which a record is known to have survived was an apparently short-lived variant of the British Union Jack, differenced with a white shield placed over the centre (Fig. 64). This was established in 1701 as a jack for ships commissioned by colonial

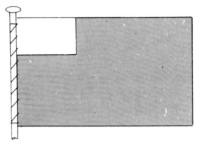

62 Massachusetts flag, 17th century

63 From a signal book of 1711 (Bibl. A 17)

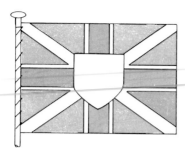

64 British colonial jack, beginning of the 18th century

governors for official business, but there is no evidence that it was ever widely used.[93]

The political ferment of the American Revolution brought about a varied range of new flags, both authorized and individualistic, which reflect the stages in the development of the new nation. Contemporary sources have been thoroughly searched by American scholars seeking for evidence on the origin of the Stars and Stripes, but in revolutionary times people do not always think of recording the details of their political symbolism which future historians may crave: there are still questions unanswered and inconsistencies in the evidence unresolved.

The first collective flag for the united colonies was the 'Continental Colours', also (less correctly) known as the 'Great Union Flag' or the 'Cambridge Flag', a flag with the British Union in the canton and a field usually with seven red and six white stripes (Plate XIV, no. 1). It is perhaps sheer coincidence that a similar flag was used by the ships of the East India Company.[94] The thirteen stripes represented the thirteen colonies; the Union reflected the fact that the colonists still maintained a theoretical loyalty to the British Crown. The 'Continental Colours' came into use in 1775 and was ceremonially hoisted by Washington on Prospect Hill, Somerville, Massachusetts, on 1 January 1776. It was used on the fleet commanded by Esek Hopkins that sailed from Philadelphia three days later. John Paul Jones asserted afterwards that he 'hoisted with my own hands, on board the *Alfred*, flagship of the Commander in Chief, the American flag, then hoisted for the first time'.[95] The flag of command used by Hopkins on this occasion is believed to have been a yellow flag with a rattlesnake on it, together with the motto DON'T TREAD ON ME. This was one of a variety of flags featuring a rattlesnake, a favourite American symbol of resistance to oppression, which were in use during the Revolution. An early representation of the 'Continental Colours' afloat is in the drawing in Figure 65, which shows the United

65 The captured American brig *Lexington*, 1777, anonymous watercolour (NMM, ms P/16/20, p 198)

66 'H.M brig *Roebuck* and her American prizes. 1778'. oil painting by Francis Holman

States brig *Lexington* after her capture by the British cutter *Alert* in September 1777. The field is shown striped red/white/blue/red/white blue/red/white/blue/red/white/blue/red.[96]

After the Declaration of Independence on 4 July 1776 a flag with the British Union was no longer appropriate and the new nation needed a new flag. Not till 14 June 1777, however, did Congress resolve that 'The Flag of the united states be 13 stripes alternate red and white, that the union be 13 stars white in a blue field representing a new constellation'. There is no record of any debates leading to this resolution, nor is there any conclusive evidence on who designed the canton of thirteen stars to replace the British Union in the canton. American folk legend associates the origin of the flag with Betsy Ross of Philadelphia, and this is partly corroborated by a note among the Pennsylvania State naval records of payment to Elizabeth Ross in May 1777, a few weeks before the flag resolution, of £14.12s.2d. 'for making ships' colours'. The main actual designer of the Stars and Stripes, however, was probably a government official called Francis Hopkinson.[97]

Although the resolution of 1777 essentially created the Stars and Stripes of modern America, the flag was not at once universally adopted in the form laid down. On land, individual units of the army continued to use their own flags and even at sea there were, for several years, substantial variations in the form of the flags used. In 1778 Benjamin Franklin and John Adams described the American flag at the request of the Neapolitan ambassador in Paris:

It is with pleasure that we acquaint your Excellency that the flag of the United States of America consists of thirteen stripes, alternately red, white, and blue; a small square in the upper angle, next the flag staff, is a blue field with thirteen white stars, denoting a new Constellation. Some of the States have vessels of war distinct from those of the United States. For example the vessels of war of the State of Massachusetts Bay have sometimes a pine tree, and those of South Carolina a rattlesnake in the middle of the thirteen stripes, but the flag of the United States, ordained by Congress, is the thirteen stripes and thirteen stars above described.[98]

67 'Stars and Stripes' captured during the British-American war of 1812-14. 193 × 345 cm

49

The existence of early versions of the Stars and Stripes with such red, white and blue stripes, as well as those made according to the Congressional resolution with red and white stripes, is corroborated by flag books published in Europe in the years following American independence, and by drawings made in 1779 at Texel in Holland of flags flown by the ships of John Paul Jones when they went into port there after Jones's celebrated fight with, and capture of, the British *Serapis*. The flag of the *Alliance*, a ship of Jones's squadron, is recorded as a Stars and Stripes with thirteen stars in five rows (3,2,3,2,3), and seven white and six red stripes. The flag on the newly captured *Serapis* was a Stars and Stripes with thirteen stars arranged in three rows

68 *(left)* Fragment of the ensign of the US frigate *Chesapeake*. 152 × 163 cm

69 The combat between the *Chesapeake* and HMS *Shannon* 1813; aquatint by Jeakes

(4,5,4) and the field striped blue/red/white/red/white/blue/red/white/red/blue/white/blue/red.[99]

European flag books and paintings of the period indicate that American merchant ships in the last quarter of the 18th century often flew not the Stars and Stripes but ensigns that were striped either red and white, or red, white and blue, without a canton of stars. Francis Holman's painting of 1778 of the British brig *Roebuck* and her American prizes shows all the prizes with ensigns striped red, white and blue, with no canton (Fig. 66). By the early 19th century the Stars and red and white Stripes had become universal on American ships, both naval and merchant: the fifteen-star flag in Figure 67 is one example – it was worn by an American coal brig taken in Long Island Sound by HMS *Borer* in the War of 1812-14.

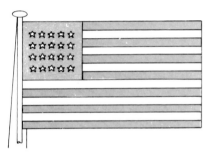

70 Pattern of Stars and Stripes established in September 1818

The thirteen stars and thirteen stripes of the 1777 flag symbolized the thirteen colonies and as new states joined the Union there was an obvious case for increasing the number. In 1795, accordingly, following the admission of Vermont and Kentucky, Congress altered the flag to have fifteen stars and fifteen stripes. This remained the pattern through the 1812 war with Great Britain despite the admission of new states. In 1816 Congress appointed a committee under Congressman Peter Wendover of New York to consider the future of the flag. Taking into account that any further increase in the number of stripes in the flag would make it less legible at a distance at sea, the committee proposed to reduce the number of stripes to the original thirteen, but to add a star for each new state. Following the Committee's report, Congress passed, on 4 April 1818 *An Act to Establish the Flag of the United States:*

Be it enacted, etc., That from and after the fourth day of July next, the flag of the United States be thirteen horizontal stripes alternate red and white; that the union have twenty stars, white in a blue field. And be it further enacted, That on the admission of every new State into the Union, one star be added to the union of the flag; and that such addition shall take effect on the fourth of July next succeeding such admission.

These rules have governed the form of the American flag ever since and the growing number of stars makes possible a rough dating for surviving flags or accurate marine paintings. The changes in the flag since 1818 have been as follows:

1818: 20 stars	1861: 34 stars
1819: 21 stars	1863: 35 stars
1820: 23 stars	1865: 36 stars
1822: 24 stars	1867: 37 stars
1836: 25 stars	1877: 38 stars
1837: 26 stars	1890: 43 stars
1845: 27 stars	1891: 44 stars
1846: 28 stars	1896: 45 stars
1847: 29 stars	1908: 46 stars
1848: 30 stars	1912: 48 stars
1851: 31 stars	1959: 49 stars
1858: 32 stars	1960: 50 stars
1859: 33 stars	

These early flag resolutions of Congress did not stipulate precise proportions or details of design. A directive of the Navy Commissioners in 1818 stipulated that the naval flag be in the proportion of 14 feet by 24, with a canton one third of the length of the flag and extending down over the top seven stripes, with the stars arranged in four parallel rows. This was not, however, legally binding on private citizens, and American shipowners in the 19th century amused themselves with arrangements of the stars in the form of an anchor, of a circle, of a single large star, of their own initials, of the letters U.S., and so on, as well as in more conventional rows.[100] Not until 1912 were precise proportions and details of arrangements officially defined.[101]

The first flag of the Confederate Southern states in the American Civil War was a modification of the Stars and Stripes. The 'Stars and Bars', adopted in March 1861, was used on land and as an ensign at sea. It was a flag striped red/white/red with at first a large square blue canton containing a circle of seven white stars. The number of stars was later in 1861 increased to thirteen, for the thirteen states participating in the Confederacy (Plate XIV, no. 6).

71 The combat between the Confederate ironclad *Merrimack* and the USS *Monitor*, 1862; engraving by Le Breton

In March 1862 the 'Stars and Bars' was flown by the bizarre Confederate steampowered ironclad *Merrimack* (alias *Virginia*) in the indecisive action with the equally extraordinary U.S.S. *Monitor*, the first battle in history between ironclads (Fig. 71). However, the 'Stars and Bars' was soon felt to be insufficiently distinct from the 'Stars and Stripes' of the Northern states and in May 1863 it was replaced by an ensign (Plate XIV, no. 7) and jack based upon the famous Confederate 'Battle Flag'. This design lasted as long as there was a Confederate navy to use it.

Since about 1800 there has been no distinction between the naval and merchant ensigns in the United States. As was traditional in the Royal Navy of Great Britain, the distinguishing flags of a ship in the United States navy are the jack, which has been since at least 1785 a flag of the starry canton (or 'Union') of the Stars and Stripes, and the commissioning pennant (U.S. 'commission pennant') which consists of a blue hoist with a row of seven white stars, and a fly divided red over white. The pennant was standardized in this form in 1934; formerly thirteen-star pennants were the norm, although seven-star versions were used for night and boat pennants.[102]

Until shortly before the American Civil War there was no flag rank in the United States navy: an officer commanding a squadron had the more modest title of 'commodore'. There is little evidence on the command flags or broad pennants used by American commodores in the Revolutionary War but by the War of 1812 the broad pennant of a commodore was blue with fifteen white stars.

In 1817 a red and white version (the latter with blue stars) were added for use by junior commodores in the presence of senior: the order of seniority was blue, red, white. In the years during and after the Civil War, when the United States Navy acquired for the first time the ranks successively of rear admiral (1862), vice admiral (1864), and admiral (1866), various experimental admirals' flags were tried. In 1876 it was finally established that the flag of an admiral, a vice admiral and a rear admiral be blue with, respectively, four, three and two white stars; a commodore was to have a blue broad pennant with a single star. The same order stipulated that there be red and white versions of the rear admiral's flag and the commodore's pennant for use by junior rear admirals and commodores in the presence of senior. During the Second World War a new rank of 'fleet admiral' was created with a five-star flag. The blue command flags with white stars are still in use as the sea-going command flags of the United States Navy flag officers.[103]

There are, of course, state flags for every one of the United States of America. These cannot be dealt with here: they are authoritatively dealt with, and beautifully illustrated, in Whitney Smith's *Flag Book of the United States*.

CHAPTER 4

Some Sea Flags Of Europe

Spain

The nation that we know as Spain developed as a result of the marriage in 1469 of Ferdinand of Aragon and Isabella of Castile. The years that followed were years of expansion: in 1492 the conquest of Granada from the Moors was completed and in 1512 Navarre was annexed to the crown of Castile. When Isabella died in 1504 her kingdom of Castile was inherited by her daughter 'Juana the Mad', who was married to Philip of Hapsburg. On Ferdinand's death in 1516 the crown of Aragon too passed to Juana, by this time a widow, and her son Charles, and the united kingdom of Spain came into being. Charles I of Spain (the Emperor Charles V of the Holy Roman Empire) also brought to the Spanish throne the Burgundian and Austrian possessions of the House of Hapsburg. These political and dynastic facts underlie the entire subsequent history of Spanish flags.

In the 16th and 17th centuries a variety of heraldic, religious, and national flags were flown on Spanish ships; the two basic motifs were the 'ragged cross' and the royal arms of Spain. The ragged cross, or saltire raguly (Plate XIV, no. 8), representing two crossed tree trunks with the branches roughly lopped, was originally a Burgundian symbol, but after 1516 it was taken up as a national emblem for Spain. Most commonly it was represented red on a white field, but it was also used in other colours and in combination with religious and heraldic motifs.

The royal arms in Spain were also commonly used as a national symbol – in contrast to their more restricted use in England. In their full form the arms of Charles I represented Castile, Leon, Aragon, Sicily, Granada, Austria, Burgundy Modern, Burgundy Ancient, Brabant, Flanders and Tyrol; they were often represented on a white flag, crowned and surrounded by the collar of the Order of the Golden Fleece, and flanked by the Pillars of Hercules with the motto PLUS ULTRA (More beyond). With the annexation of Portugal under Philip II in 1581 a shield with the arms of Portugal was added; it

remained in the Spanish royal arms, despite the loss of Portugal in 1640, till 1685. These are the arms represented in many of the flag books of the late 17th and early 18th centuries (Plate XIV, no. 9; Fig. 72). The quarters are as follows: 1: Castile quartering Leon; 2: Aragon impaling Sicily; between 1 and 2, in base, the pomegranate of Granada; 3: Austria over Burgundy Ancient; 4: Burgundy Modern over Brabant; the upper inescutcheon represents Portugal, the lower Flanders impaling Tyrol.

72 Spanish royal flag, from Allard (Bibl. A 9)

In the 16th century the ragged cross, the royal arms, and religious paintings such as the Virgin, the Crucifixion, and St James of Compostela, were used in various combinations. Two fragmentary flags of the end of the 16th century or the beginning of the 17th, preserved in the Rijksmuseum, Amsterdam, have the royal arms, crowned and with the collar of the Golden Fleece, on a white field, between pillars and PLUS ULTRA: another fragment apparently had the simple quarterings of Castile and Leon in a crowned and collared shield with a red ragged cross behind and the pillars and PLUS ULTRA at the sides.[104]

The flags flown on particular occasions are sporadically recorded. Columbus recorded that his

73 'The Battle of Lepanto, 1571', anonymous oil painting

flags for his epoch-making voyage of 1492 included 'the royal flag' ... 'two flags with a green cross, which the Admiral had on all the ships as a signal, with an F and a Y; above each letter a crown... One letter was on each side of the cross.' The F and Y were in honour of Ferdinand and Isabella, patrons of the voyage.[105] The Spanish, Venetian and other galleys that took part in the battle of Lepanto in 1571 against the Turks used a prodigious variety of heraldic and religious flags, including some specially consecrated ones.[106] The flags used by the ill-fated Armada of 1588 are poorly recorded. The near-contemporary pictures of the Armada, such as the one in Plate V, usually show a combination of religious and heraldic flags, flags with the ragged cross, and striped flags, particularly in the prime heraldic colours of Spain, yellow and red. The prominence of images of the Virgin and the Crucifixion reflects the Counter-Reformation crusading zeal which inspired the Armada.[107]

In the 17th century religious images became less common on Spanish flags. The ragged cross was widely used as a national emblem and by merchant ships, while the king's ships tended to use either the full royal arms in a white flag or the simplified version quartering Castile and Leon.

In 1700 the Hapsburg dynasty on the Spanish throne gave way to a new Bourbon-Anjou dynasty in the person of Philip IV. The arms were rearranged and a large central escutcheon with three fleurs-de-lis added. In 1759 the arms were altered again to incorporate the six blue fleurs-de-lis of the Farnese family (to represent the Duchy of Parma) and the roundels (five red, the topmost blue with three gold fleurs-de-lis) of the Medici (to represent the Grand Duchy of Tuscany). The royal arms lasted in this form with minor modifications until the Spanish Civil War in the 1930s.[108]

Meanwhile, however, the flags of the Spanish navy were comprehensively revised. In 1732 the following royal proclamation was issued:

The King having decided that the fleet be divided into three squadrons and that each of them should have its home port in one of the three sections established in Spain, viz. Cadiz, Ferrol and Cartagena, His Majesty has decreed that in order that each squadron may be distinguished by its flags and ensigns, all the

74 From the *Neptune François* (Bibl. A 10)

ships, of whatever squadron, are to have large white stern ensigns with the royal arms as at present. The ships based at Cadiz should use for their emblem for square flags, cornets, cocks' tails, pennants, jacks, boat and barge flags, the aforesaid shield of the royal arms on white. The ships based at Ferrol are to use in all the said flags, jacks and boat and barge flags the cross of Burgundy on white with four anchors in the corners of the square formed by the arms of the cross. The ships based at Cartagena are to use in the said flags, jacks and boat and barge flags the simplified shield of the royal arms, with the castles and the lions in the approved form on a purple ground with four anchors at the corners.[109]

In 1785, on the grounds that the white flags were liable to be confused at a distance at sea with other white flags, such as those used by the French navy and the white squadron of the British navy, it was decided to introduce a completely new set of naval flags. A number of designs were submitted, mostly based on the traditional red and yellow colours of Spain. On 28 May 1785 a decree announced the king's decision:

In order to avoid the inconvenience and difficulties which experience has shown can be caused by the national flag used by my navy and other Spanish forces being mistaken over great distances or in the absence of wind for those of other nations, I have resolved that henceforth my warships shall use a flag divided lengthwise into three stripes, of which the top and bottom ones shall be red and each one quarter of the total width, the central stripe to be yellow bearing upon it my royal arms reduced to the two quarterings of Castile and Leon with the royal crown above; and the pennant with the same three stripes and the shield on a yellow square at the hoist. The other ships are to use the same colours, without the shield, the middle stripe being yellow and one third of the whole width of the flag and each of the remaining parts being divided into two stripes of equal width of red and yellow. . .[110]

The 1785 flags are illustrated in Plates XIV, no. 10, and XV, nos. 11 and 12.

Since 1785, with some variations, arrangements of red, yellow, and red have remained in use, with the exception of the period of the Second Republic, 1931-6, when a tricolour of red, yellow, and purple

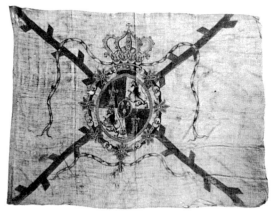

75 Spanish flag, thought to have been captured at the siege of Gibraltar, 1782; on loan from R.G. Franklin. 229 × 279 cm

76 Spanish ensign of the 1785 pattern. 216 × 302 cm

was adopted instead. At present the national flag, which is used by naval vessels, is red, yellow, red, with the shield of the arms of Spain in the yellow stripe (Plate XV, no. 13).[111] The merchant ensign, introduced in 1928, is of the same pattern, without the coat of arms. The naval jack is a square flag bearing quarterly Castile, Leon, Aragon, Navarre (Plate XV, no. 14).

The Netherlands

The origin of the modern nation of the Netherlands and of the Dutch national tricolour of red, white, and blue (Plate XV, no. 16) goes back to the beginning of the long war of independence against the Spanish crown. From about 1572 rebel ships flew a tricolour of orange over white over blue. This flag which was known as the 'Prince flag' with reference to the great leader of the developing nation, William the Silent, Prince of Orange, came to be accepted as the principal national flag of the United Provinces. Between about 1630 and 1660 the upper stripe came usually to be red rather than orange.[112]

In the 17th century, the great age of Dutch sea power and of Dutch sea painting, the plain tricolour was widely used as an ensign and as a jack and naval command flag. Warships had tricolour pennants (Plate XV, no. 19), often plain, but sometimes shown in paintings with a coat of arms or a badge at the hoist. There were many variants of the basic tricolour in use: as was noted in 1671, people decorated the white stripe 'in whatever way they pleased'.[113] Some flags had coats of arms added; others had letters or monograms, like the VOC of the East India Company (Verenigde Oost-indische Compagnie) or the GWC of the West India Company (Geoctrooieerde West-indische Compagnie).[114] There are paintings showing tricolours ornamented with orange branches in token of support for the House of Orange, and of whaling ships with a whale in the white stripe.[115] There were also various multiple-striped versions of the orange(red), white, blue colours.

The Dutch fleets of the three naval wars with England in 1652-4, 1665-7 and 1672-4 were assembled from ships belonging to the five independent Admiralties – Amsterdam, Rotterdam, the North Quarter of Holland, Zeeland, and Friesland – and had numerous flag officers and varying numbers of squadrons. The flag arrangements distinguishing the squadrons and the Admiralties varied from fleet to fleet and were often extremely elaborate. The

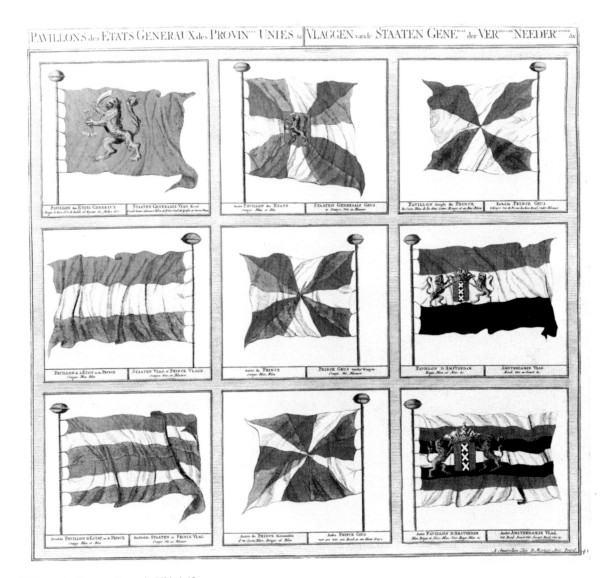

77 From the *Neptune François* (Bibl. A 10)

basic principle was the same as that adopted in the English navy, that an admiral's flag flew at the main, a vice admiral's flag at the fore, and a rear admiral's at the mizzen, but it was complicated by the fact that flag officers sometimes flew their flags to correspond not with their post in the fleet but with their regular rank in their own Admiralty. When a fleet was divided into three squadrons the squadrons were distinguished by the mastheads at which the ships flew their pennants – the centre squadron at the main, the van at the fore, and the rear at the mizzen. When there were more than three squadrons further distinctions were made: at the battle of Lowestoft in

1665, for instance, there were seven squadrons in the Dutch fleet, three distinguished by the masthead at which their pennants flew, the other four by the use of special variously coloured small masthead flags or vanes. By the time of the Four Days Battle the following year the fleet had been re-organized by De Ruyter into three squadrons with pennants at different mastheads; the different Admiralties to which ships belonged were indicated by the use of tricolours, multiple-striped flags and town flags in different combinations as ensigns and jacks. At the Third Dutch War Battle of Solebay in 1672 the fleet was again in three squadrons and all the ensigns,

57

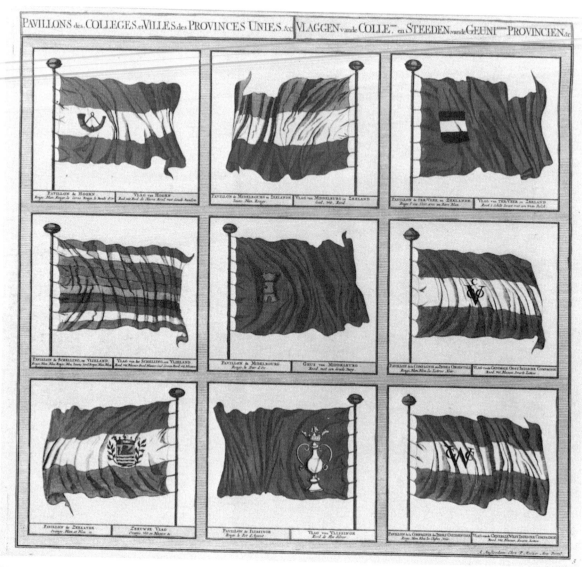

78 From the *Neptune François* (Bibl. A 10)

jacks and command flags in the fleet were the simple tricolour. At the Battle of Texel the following year the Amsterdam squadron commanded by Cornelis Tromp was distinguished by multiple striped ensigns and command flags (Fig. 79).

The evidence for the flag arrangement on both sides during the wars is visual as well as documentary. The Elder Van de Velde was present at several of the battles in a specially provided vessel and his drawings done on the spot and shortly afterwards are primary evidence. But even with such an apparently impeccable source there are sometimes inconsistencies between the different illustrations of a single battle. The drawings tend to be more reliable as sources than the subsequent oil paintings or grisailles: two rich collections of drawings by the Van de Veldes are in the National Maritime Museum and the Boymans-van Beuningen Museum in Rotterdam; both have been fully and authoritatively catalogued.[116]

The distinctive flag of the 'States General' of the seven United Provinces consisted of a lion – an emblem found in the coat of arms of several of the individual provinces – holding a sword and a bunch

58

79 The Battle of Texel, 1673, drawing by the Younger Van de Velde (detail), showing the multiple-striped ensigns and command flags of Cornelis Tromp's squadron

of seven arrows representing the seven provinces. At first (Plate XV, no. 17) the colours were those of the flag of Holland, the dominant province in the union, a red lion on a yellow field. Soon after the middle of the 17th century the colours were reversed (Plate XV, no. 18).[117] The flag was particularly used by yachts and other vessels belonging to the States General.

At some time after the end of the Third Dutch War was apparently introduced a new range of naval jacks in which the red, white and blue were arranged in a 'gyronny' pattern radiating from the centre. These jacks (Fig. 77) are illustrated by van der Dussen and Allard (Bibliography A8, A9), and in later flag books, but it has so far proved impossible to find contemporary illustrations of them in use and it is open to doubt whether they were ever much used. In 1931 the gyronny arrangement was revived as a naval jack (Plate XV, no. 21); gyronny flags are also sometimes used by Dutch pleasure craft.

Through the 18th century the tricolour was

80 A Dutch ship off Flushing; detail from an anonymous oil painting c 1720; the ship wears the 'vase' jack of Flushing (compare fig. 78)

81 Canton from a 'Batavian Republic' ensign, beginning of the 19th century. 101 × 184 cm

unchallenged as the national flag for merchant ships and warships until the Netherlands passed under French domination after the French Revolution, and the so-called 'Batavian Republic' was formed. On 14 February 1796 it was ordered that the naval (but not the merchant) flags be altered by the insertion of a panel containing 'a representation of a female figure in a graceful attitude seated on a patch of greenery, and holding a spear on which is the Cap of Liberty . . . At her feet a lion in a sitting or rather reclining position with its head turned sideways and with a fierce and grim expression on its face. . .'[118] A full range of naval flags and pennants featuring this device were used by the navy of the Republic in the years that followed (Plate XV, no. 20). The National Maritime Museum has the blue command flag of Vice Admiral de Winter[119] taken at the battle of Camperdown in 1797 (Plate XIII). The Batavian device was abandoned after the Republic gave way to a monarchy in 1806.

France

In the 16th century the two primary national symbols on French flags were the fleur-de-lis and the white cross. The royal arms, known to heraldry as 'France Modern', were three golden fleurs-de-lis on blue. They had been altered from the older form, *semé* of fleurs-de-lis ('France Ancient') towards the end of the 14th century, but flags and streamers *semé* of fleurs-de-lis, as well as flags incorporating the royal arms, continued to be used. The white cross corresponded to the English red cross of St George: it was a national rather than a royal emblem and was used on flags of various designs both on land and sea. Its field was often, but not always, blue.

In the first half of the 17th century the French sailing navy began to use white flags, white being the colour associated with the Crown. The Jesuit Fournier in his *Hydrographie* of 1643 wrote that 'France uses argent, or white, without any device for

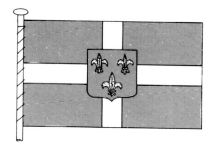

82 Official design of French merchant flag from 1661

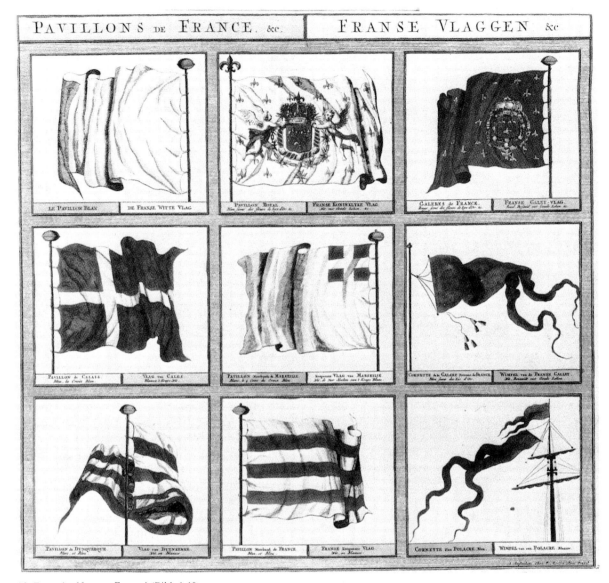

83 From the *Neptune François* (Bibl. A 10)

ordinary use . . . At present in France every squadron uses 'vanes' [*flouettes*] and ensigns of their provincial colours, with the white flag at the main. Ships not belonging to the King are required to use only a blue flag with a white cross in the middle'.[120] In 1661 an order was issued banning merchant ships from using white colours. Just as English merchant ships were illegally wearing the 'King's Jack', French merchant ships were apparently using white flags 'pour en tirer avantage dans leur commerce et Navigation'; by the order they were to use only 'l'ancien Pavillon de la nation Françoise', a blue flag with a white cross, with the royal arms overall (Fig. 82).[121] A further order of 1670 insisted that all the flags and pennants of naval ships should be white, rather than distinguished by the devices of the various provinces; nor was the red battle flag that had been in use to be used any more. The following detailed regulations, incorporating and revising earlier orders, were issued in 1689:

Only the flagship of the Admiral, with the Admiral on board, is to fly the white flag at the main. The vice admiral is to fly it at the fore; the rear admiral or senior lieutenant general, or the commodore [*chef d'escadre*] performing his function, at the mizzen.

The commodores are to fly a white broad pennant [*cornette blanche*] at the mizzen ...

... The command flags are to have the fly one quarter longer than the hoist. The broad pennants are to have the fly four times the hoist; they are to be split in the middle for two-thirds of their length, and the tails are to be pointed.

The flags of the Admiral, vice admiral and rear admiral, and the broad pennants are only to be flown in company, viz. the Admiral when accompanied by twenty warships, the vice and rear admirals by twelve of at least thirty-six guns, and the broad pennants by five.

Vice admirals, lieutenant generals and commodores in command of fewer ships are to fly an ordinary pennant unless they have a written permit from His Majesty to use a flag or a broad pennant.

When several commodores are together in a single division or squadron, only the senior is to fly a broad pennant: the others are to have an ordinary pennant.

Captains in command of more than one ship are to have a white pennant at the main half the breadth of a broad pennant, the fly of at least ten ells [approximately twelve metres].

On His Majesty's ships no other flag, pennant or ensign than white is to be flown, whether under way or in battle; red and other colours are to be used only for signals ...

... Merchant ships are to wear the blue stern ensign with a white cross throughout, and the arms of His Majesty overall, or any other distinction they think fit, as long as their ensign is not plain white ...

... The commander of a fleet of merchant vessels under way may fly a white pennant at the main; it must be taken down when in sight of any of His Majesty's warships.

On holidays and days of celebration merchant ships may be decorated with pennants and other ornaments of any colour except white.[122]

The official French merchant flag, blue with a white cross and the royal arms, was apparently not popular, and French merchant ships at the end of the 17th century and in the 18th commonly used either the banned white colours, or provincial flags. Desroches in his *Dictionnaire des termes propres de marine* (1687) noted that French merchant ships 'use different combinations of white and blue'.[123] French provincial and port flags, most of which were white and blue, feature prominently in flag books of the period.[124]

Alongside the plain white ensigns, jacks, command flags, pennants and vanes that were normal in the French sailing navy, there existed more elaborate variants. Some ship portraits and numerous flag books (Fig. 83) illustrate the *'Pavillon Royal'*, a sumptuous white flag *semé* of fleurs-de-lis with the royal arms, crowned, surrounded by the collars of the Orders of St Michael and the Holy Ghost, and supported by two angels. This flag was restricted to the King and the royal family.[125]

The 1689 regulations described a scheme of distinguishing between flag officers in which all the flags were white: the Admiral had his white flag at the main, the vice admiral at the fore, and the rear admiral at the mizzen; commodores had white broad pennants. Later on, however, large fleets were sometimes divided by colour: the flag officers of the centre had white command flags; those of the van had flags divided horizontally white over blue; those of the rear had blue flags of command.[126] The ensigns however, were all white: the French navy did not carry the principal of squadronal distinction by colour as far as the British.

The paragraphs above apply only to the French sailing navy of the Atlantic. The galley fleet based in the Mediterranean was until 1748 quite distinct and had a sumptuous range of flags in which red was the dominant colour. The standard of the *Galère Reale* was red, *semé* of fleurs-de-lis, with the crowned and collared royal arms. Figure 84 is a late-17th-century engraving of the *Galère Reale* which gives some idea of the lavish adornment of the Mediterranean galley fleets.

White flags remained characteristic of French sailing ships until the French Revolution. In 1790 a new set of naval flags was introduced by order of the Revolutionary Assembly. The new ensign was white, with a canton consisting of a tricolour of three equal vertical stripes, red to the hoist, white, blue, within a blue and red border (Plate XVI, no. 23); the jack (Plate XVI, no. 24) consisted of this canton alone; the pennant was white, with the same canton occupying the hoist.[127] This lasted until 1794, when the white field was abolished and the order of the colours reversed, thus virtually producing the Tricolour of modern France. This was used at the battle of the 'Glorious First of June', 1794: although there had not been enough bunting at Brest to re-equip the whole fleet, the command flag of Admiral Villaret de Joyeuse in the *Montagne* was a Tricolour of the new pattern.[128] In the remaining battles of the Revolutionary and Napoleonic Wars the French navy used the Tricolour as ensign, command flag, and jack, and the pennant was similarly divided blue/white/red (Plate

84 The Royal Galley of the French Mediterranean galley fleet at the end of the 17th century; engraved by C. Randon for H.S. de Passebon, *Plan de Plusieurs Bâtimens de Mer,* c 1700

85 HMS *Marlborough* engaging two French ships at the Battle of the First of June 1794; drawing by Nicholas Pocock. The French ships are shown with ensigns and pennants of the 1790 pattern

XVI, no. 25). The white colours of the French monarchy were re-introduced in 1814 and lasted, except for a brief period in 1815 when Napoleon restored the Tricolour, until the fall of the monarchy in 1830. Since that date the Tricolour has remained almost unchallenged, the national flag of France on land and sea. Although the blue, white and red bands are of equal width in the national flag, the proportions of the version of the Tricolour officially established for use as a sea-going ensign are now: blue 30 per cent of the length of the flag, white 33 per cent, and red 37 per cent (Plate XVI, no. 26).

86 French flagship, around 1700 (from the 1716 edition of Allard's flagbook, Bibl. A9)

1

2

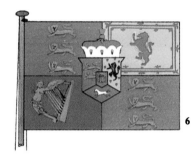

3

4

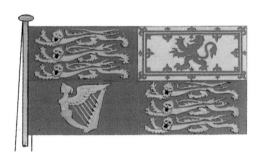

5

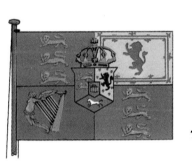

6

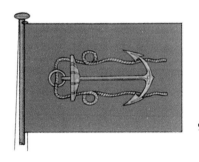

7

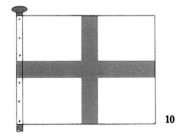

8

Plate I   British sea flags

1   English 'Royal Standard' c 1407-1603
2   British 'Royal Standard' 1603-89;
     1702-7
3   British 'Royal Standard' 1689-1702
4   British 'Royal Standard' 1707-14
5   British 'Royal Standard' 1714-1800
6   British 'Royal Standard' 1801-16
7   British 'Royal Standard' 1816-37
8   British 'Royal Standard', modern
9   Flag of the Lord High Admiral, from
     17th century (with variations)
     The current version is usually on a
     crimson rather than scarlet ground
     The run of the cable has varied several
     times during the history of the flag.
10   Flag of St George
11   Flag of St Andrew

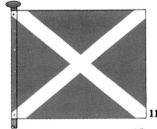

9

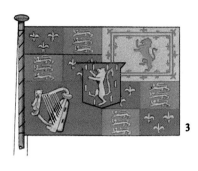

10

11

65

Plate II British sea flags

12 Union flag and jack 1606-1800
13 Commonwealth jack and command flag c 1649-58
14 Union flag and jack 1658-60
15 Striped ensign typical of period c 1600-30
16 Striped ensign typical of period c 1600-30
17 Red ensign c 1620-1707
18 Scottish red ensign 17th-18th century
19 Red ensign 1707-1800
20 Normal form of white ensign 1707-1800 (see also fig. 25)
21 Blue ensign 1707-1800

12

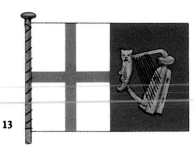

13

14

15

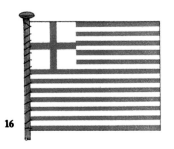

16

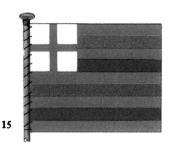

17

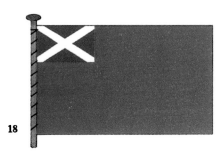

18

19

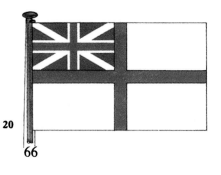

20

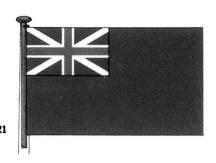

21

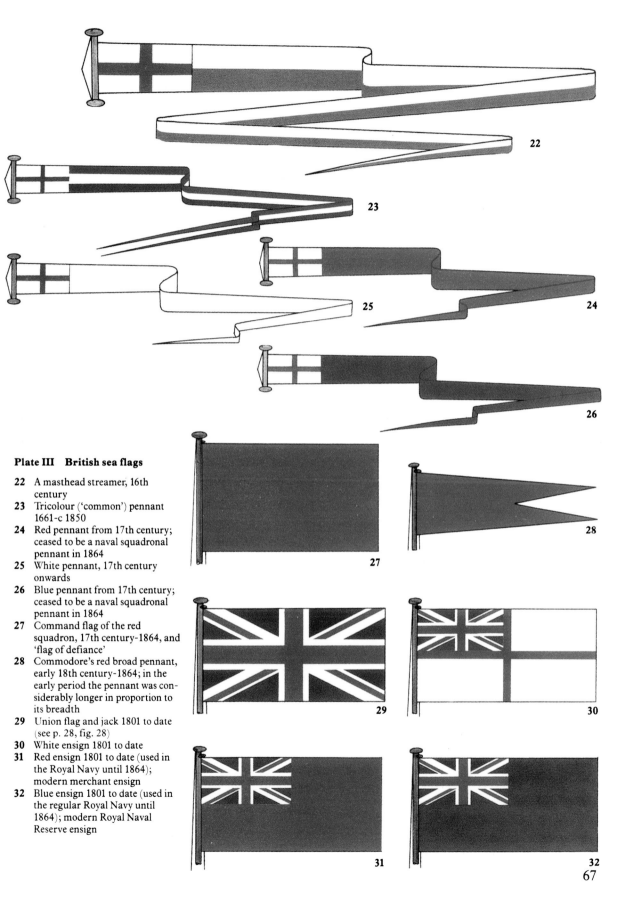

Plate III British sea flags

22 A masthead streamer, 16th century

23 Tricolour ('common') pennant 1661-c 1850

24 Red pennant from 17th century; ceased to be a naval squadronal pennant in 1864

25 White pennant, 17th century onwards

26 Blue pennant from 17th century; ceased to be a naval squadronal pennant in 1864

27 Command flag of the red squadron, 17th century-1864, and 'flag of defiance'

28 Commodore's red broad pennant, early 18th century-1864; in the early period the pennant was considerably longer in proportion to its breadth

29 Union flag and jack 1801 to date (see p. 28, fig. 28)

30 White ensign 1801 to date

31 Red ensign 1801 to date (used in the Royal Navy until 1864); modern merchant ensign

32 Blue ensign 1801 to date (used in the regular Royal Navy until 1864); modern Royal Naval Reserve ensign

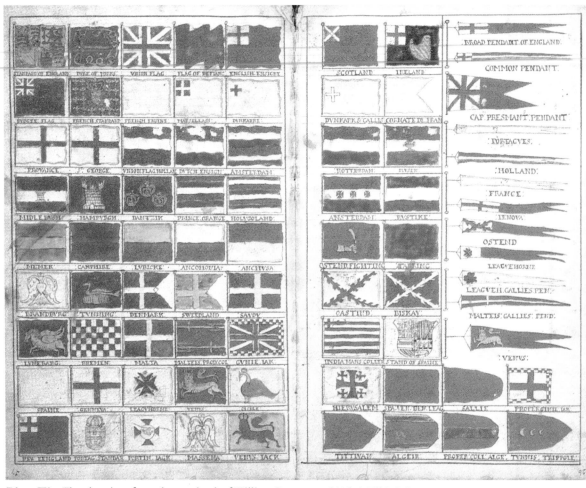

Plate IV Flag drawings from the notebook of William Downman 1685-6 (Bibl. A6)

Plate V 'The Spanish Armada in the English Channel 1588', anonymous gouache, c. 1610.

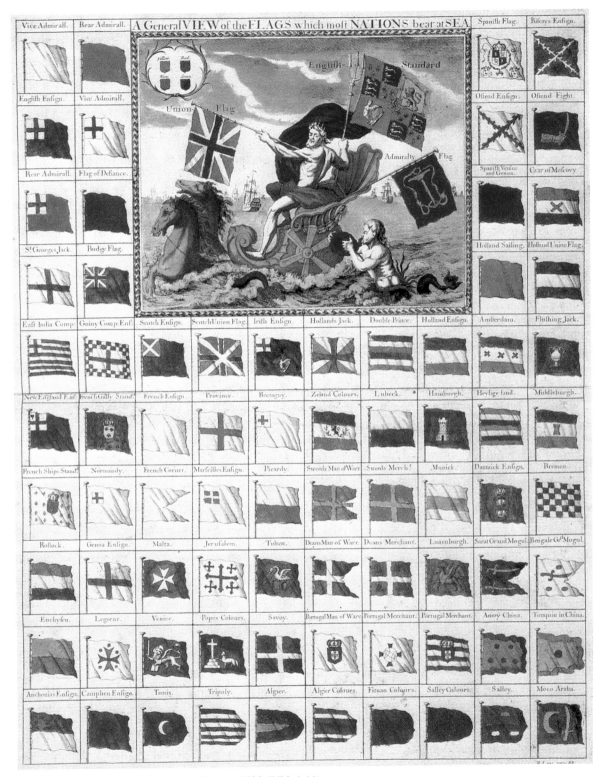

Plate VI Flag chart published by B. Lens c. 1700 (Bibl. A 11)

69

Plate VII (*above*)
Union Flag flown by HMS *Queen Charlotte* at the Battle of the First of June, 1794; on loan from Miss J. Reynolds. This was the command flag of Lord Howe, who was Acting Admiral of the Fleet. 366 × 518 cm.

Plate VIII (*right*)   Flag chart published by R.H. Laurie (Bibl. A 29), 1842. An early Victorian issue of Laurie's flag sheet. This was one of the many flag charts published in the first half of the 19th century. They were produced as charts, bound up with atlases or encyclopaedias, made into flag books and even printed onto silk headscarves. This chart, while not perfect, is freer from blunders than many.

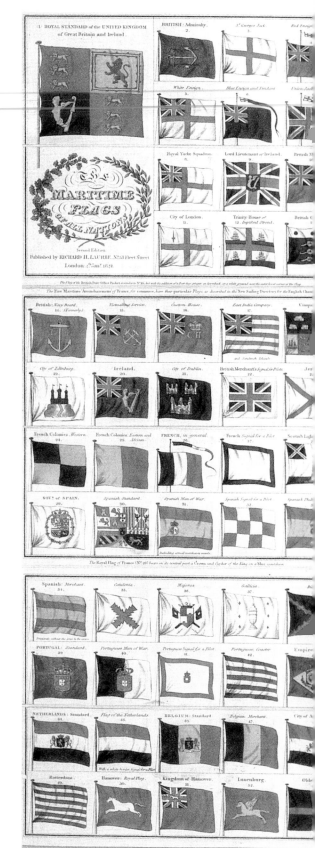

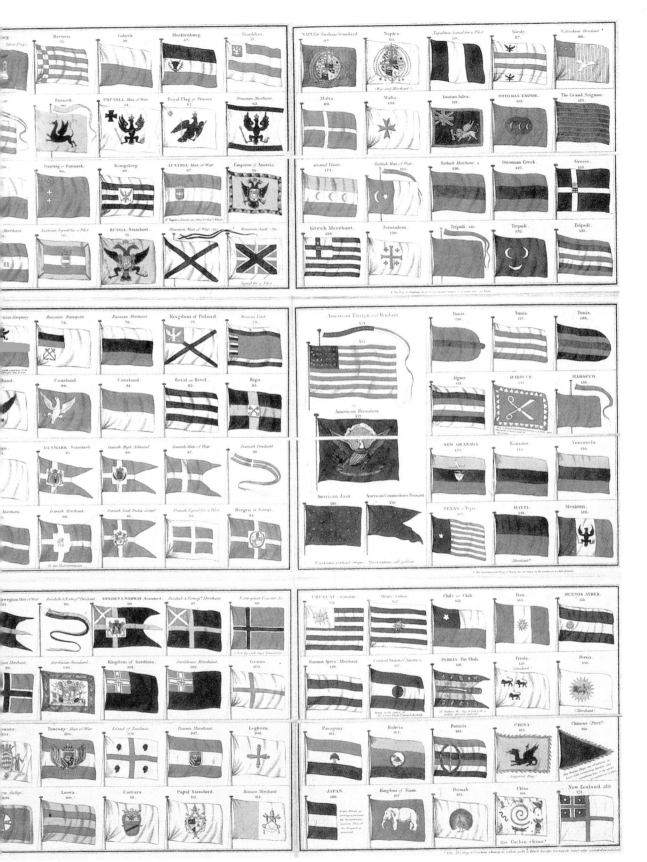

Plate IX 'The Relief of Barcelona, 1706', oil painting by H. Vale showing a combined Anglo-Dutch fleet.

Plate X 'The Battle of Camperdown, 1797', oil painting by Thomas Whitcombe; compare Plate XIII.

Plate XI *(above)*
English command flag c. 1652-4.
465 × 625 cm

Plate XII *(right)*
Armorial banner of Frederick,
Duke of York and Albany, second
son of George III, c. 1790-1800.
The wheel in the fourth quarter
represents the bishopric of
Osnabruck. 305 × 488 cm.

Plate XIII
Command flag of the Dutch Vice Admiral de Winter
at the Battle of Camperdown, 1797 (see Plate X); on
loan from the Trustees of the Duncan Collection.
229 × 396 cm.

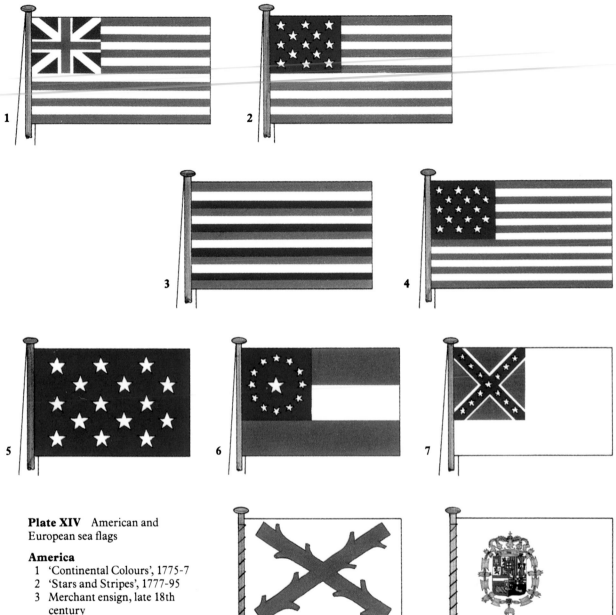

Plate XIV American and European sea flags

America
1 'Continental Colours', 1775-7
2 'Stars and Stripes', 1777-95
3 Merchant ensign, late 18th century
4 Stars and Stripes 1795-1818
5 Naval jack 1795-1818
6 Confederate ensign 1861-3
7 Confederate ensign 1863-5

Spain
8 'Ragged cross' flag, 16th-18th century
9 Royal flag/naval ensign, 17th century
10 Naval ensign 1785

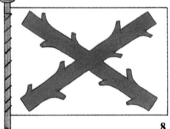

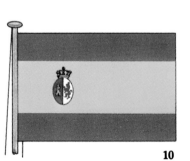

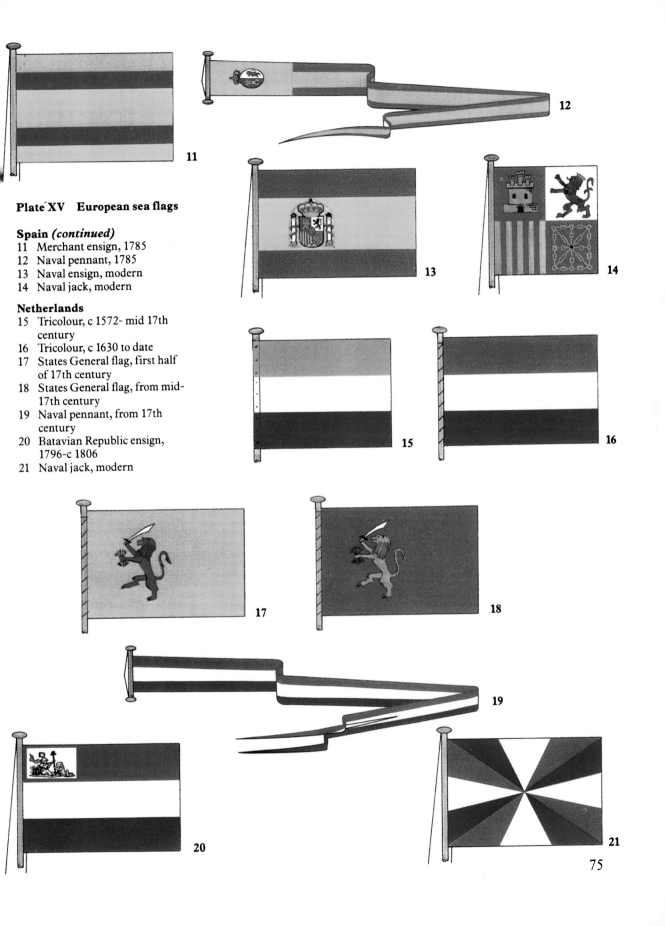

Plate XV   European sea flags

Spain *(continued)*

11 Merchant ensign, 1785
12 Naval pennant, 1785
13 Naval ensign, modern
14 Naval jack, modern

Netherlands

15 Tricolour, c 1572- mid 17th century
16 Tricolour, c 1630 to date
17 States General flag, first half of 17th century
18 States General flag, from mid-17th century
19 Naval pennant, from 17th century
20 Batavian Republic ensign, 1796-c 1806
21 Naval jack, modern

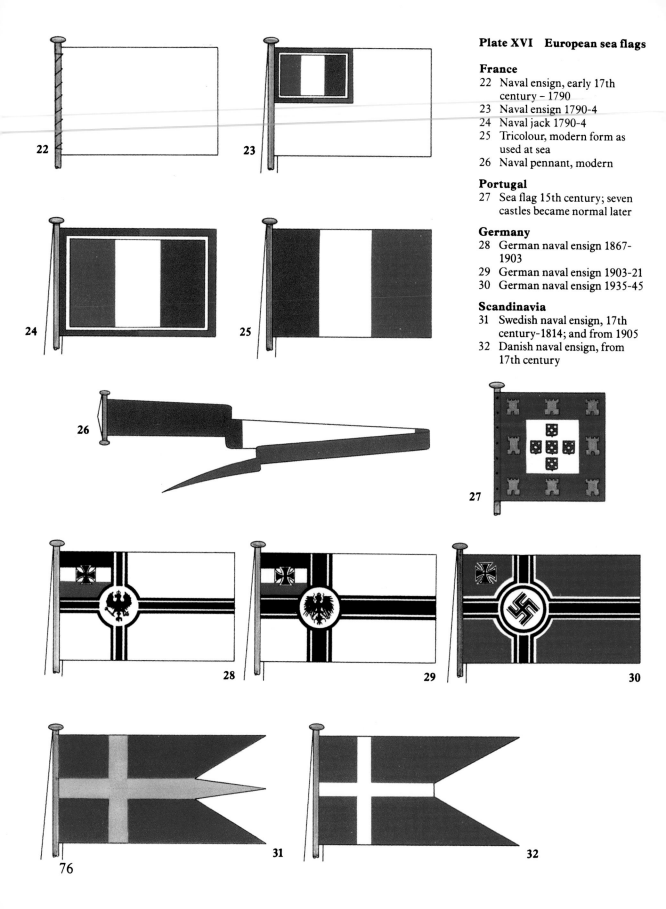

Plate XVI European sea flags

France
22 Naval ensign, early 17th century – 1790
23 Naval ensign 1790-4
24 Naval jack 1790-4
25 Tricolour, modern form as used at sea
26 Naval pennant, modern

Portugal
27 Sea flag 15th century; seven castles became normal later

Germany
28 German naval ensign 1867-1903
29 German naval ensign 1903-21
30 German naval ensign 1935-45

Scandinavia
31 Swedish naval ensign, 17th century-1814; and from 1905
32 Danish naval ensign, from 17th century

CHAPTER 5

Flag Signalling

The Royal Navy

Outside the Mediterranean (where the handling of fleets of galleys required a certain tactical sophistication) naval tactics in the Middle Ages were generally primitive, and there was no need for any elaborate system of communication by flags between ships in the fleet. An admiral who wanted to communicate with the captains of ships in his fleet would normally call them aboard his flagship: the one flag signal that regularly appears in early English fleet instructions is a 'Banner of Council': Thomas Audley's orders of 1530, for instance, laid down that 'Whensoever, and at all tymes the Admyrall doth shote of a pece of Ordnance, and set up his Banner of Council on Starrborde bottocke of his Shippe, everie shipps capten shall with spede go aborde the Admyrall to know his will';[129] and Frobisher's fleet orders for his expedition of 1578 stipulated that 'upon the sight of an Ensigne in the mast of the Admirall (a piece being shot off) the whole fleet shall repaire to the Admirall, to understand such conference as the Generall is to have with them.'[130] There are occasional mentions in early sources of other types of communication involving flags, firing guns, raising and lowering certain sails, and hanging out lights at night, but in general communication between English ships until the 17th century was by word of mouth. There were, however, certain internationally understood conventions, particularly the use of a red flag (later known as the 'bloody flag' or 'flag of defiance') as a sign of battle, and a white flag as a flag of truce.[131]

The three Dutch Wars (1652-4, 1665-7, 1672-4) with their succession of pitched battles between enormous English and Dutch fleets, provided a stimulus to the rapid development of systematic naval tactics and communications. Several sets of instructions were issued for the conduct of particular fleets, beginning with instructions issued by the Generals at Sea (Blake, Deane and Monck) in March 1653 and culminating in the first printed volume of *Sailing and Fighting Instructions*, issued on the authority of James, Duke of York, Lord High Admiral, in 1673 (Fig. 86).[132] These instructions allowed an admiral to convey various orders to his fleet by hoisting flags in different positions. The flags used were chiefly the ensigns, standard, jack, pen-

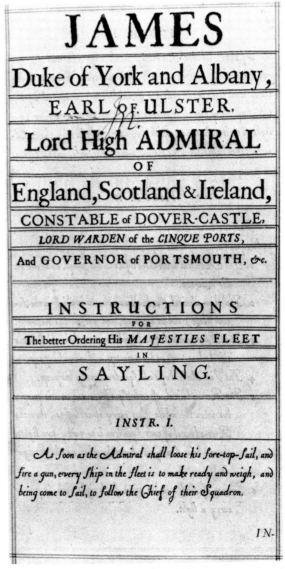

87 James Duke of York's *Instructions*, 1673

88 'An English flagship making the signal to anchor', oil painting by Peter Monamy (1681-1749)

89 *(below, left)* From Millan's *Signals*, 1746-8 (Bibl. A 21)

90 *(below, right)* From Greenwood's signal book, 1714

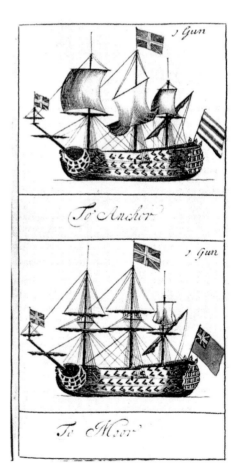

Signal. 7.   Signal. 8.

Place	A.	Sig	G	P	Significat.ᵃ	
Main top maſt head {wᵗʰ a Pendᵗ undʳ					Red Sqᵈ to draw into a line	{head {breaſt
Fore top maſt head {wᵗʰ a Pendᵗ undʳ	30 F	1	26	V.A.	Red & his Diviſⁿˢ to draw into a line	{head {breaſt
Mizen top maſt head {wᵗʰ Pendᵗ undʳ				R.A		{head {breaſt
Fore / Mizen} top maſt head	{14 {15} S	1	{5 {6}	Comᵈʳ 2ᵈ 3ᵈ Poſt	to ſend out Ships to Chace	
Mizen Peak	Addⁿ		2		To Exᵗ ſtrange Shᵖˢ paſsᵍ thro ᵍ Fleet	
Main top maſt head {wᵗʰ Pendᵗ undʳ				{Comᵈ ᵍ 2 Poſt	& his Diviſⁿ to draw into a line a	{head {breaſt
Fore top maſt head {Pendᵗ undʳ	30 F	1	26	{V. {Adᵗ {R} White		{head {breaſt
Mizen top maſthead {Pendᵗ under						{head {breaſt
Flagſtaff atʳ fore top maſthead			34		Ships Chaceᵈ S.W. to come in to ᵍ Fleet	
Miz.Shᵖ Partᵈ Ship Signal	S	1	34		Partᵈ Ship to Chace to ᵍ S.W.	
Enſign Staff	20		6		Prepare to Anchor	

DAY SIGNALS,   without COLOURS

| Prepare to Sail | 1 | 1 | 3 | Fore } |

nants and command flags carried for normal use, but there were also a few flags used solely for signalling purposes. The meaning of a signal depended on which part of the ship the flag was hoisted on.

In the years following the *Instructions* were continuously revised and extended by various admirals. In 1703 the *Instructions for the directing and governing Her Majesty's fleet in sailing and fighting* were printed in a standardized form which was to remain in use until the 1780s They were issued by individual flag officers, who frequently issued additional instructions and signals for use by the fleets under their command. At first these were added in manuscript in issued copies of the *Instructions;* later there were separate volumes of officially issued *Additional Instructions*. After the middle of the 18th century the number of additional instructions increased rapidly, with a corresponding increase in the number of special signal flags required.

Typical of the flag signals to be found in the *Instructions* are the following:

When the Admiral would have the Fleet prepare to anchor he will hoist an Ensign, strip'd Red, White and Blue, on the Ensign-staff and fire a Gun; then every Flag-Ship in the Fleet is to make the same Signal. [Compare Figs. 88-90].

As soon as the Admiral shall put abroad an Union Flag in the Mizenshrouds, and fire a Gun, all the Captains in the Fleet are to come aboard the Admiral's ship; if the same Signal, and a Weft with the Ensign, a Lieutenant of each ship is to come on Board.

As soon as the Admiral shall hoist a Red flag on the Flagstaff at the Fore-top-mast-head, and fire a Gun, every Ship in the Fleet is to use their utmost Endeavour to engage the Enemy in the Order the Admiral has prescribed unto them.

The flag signals given in the *Instructions* were, generally speaking, a one-way communication system: they were designed to enable an admiral to convey orders to the ships of his fleet, rather than for the individual ships of the fleet to pass messages to the admiral or to each other. Only flagships usually carried a full set of the flags needed for signalling. Signals could be directed to a particular ship or group of ships by a system of distinguishing pennants.

To serve as a 'ready reference' to the signals in the *Instructions* various kinds of illustrated 'signal books' for use by 'private ships' were produced[133]. A large volume in the National Maritime Museum, dated 1711, is one of the earliest signal books known; it has handsome coloured drawings of ships making signals from the *Instructions* (Fig. 91).[134] In 1714 a printed signal book on the same lines, but pocket sized, was

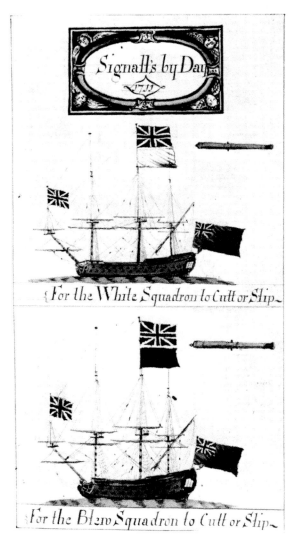

91 From an English manuscript signal book, dated 1711 (Bibl. A 17)

issued by Jonathan Greenwood: each of the small pages has two engravings of a flagship signalling (Fig. 90). It was a handy book and was widely used.[135]

A different kind of signal book arranged the instructions flag by flag, with drawings of the flags at the top of each page or in thumb-index form down the sides.[136] In 1746-8 a printed pocket signal book on this basis was published by J. Millan; this useful handbook includes a variety of information for naval officers (Fig. 89).

By the time of the American War of Independence the *Sailing and Fighting Instructions* with their ever-growing accretions of *Additional Instructions* were becoming unwieldy as more and more flags

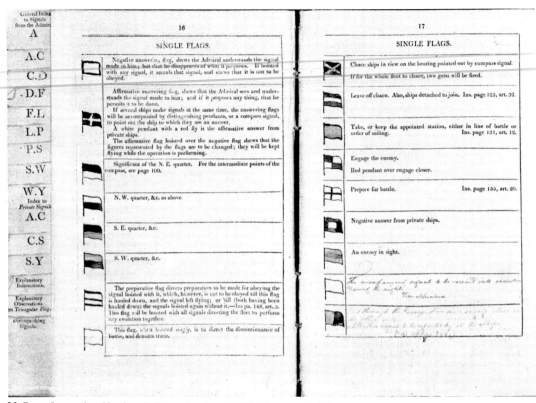

92 Pages from a signal book probably used on board HMS *Victory* at Trafalgar (NMM, SIG/B/76)

were brought into use. The first step in the development of a new approach was taken in 1776 when Admiral Lord Howe issued his fleet on the North American Station with a new book entitled *Signal Book for the Ships of War*, together with an accompanying *Instructions for the Conduct of the Ships of War, Explanatory of, and relative to the Signals contained in the Signal-Book herewith delivered.*[137] In these books Howe revised and simplified the range of flags used in the traditional *Instructions* and *Additional Instructions* and prepared the way for the development of a more flexible and comprehensive system of flag signalling. In the years following, he and a number of other officers (notably, until his death in the sinking of the *Royal George* in 1782, Rear Admiral Richard Kempenfelt) experimented with new systems of signalling, in which a fairly small number of signal flags could be used to make a greater range of signals. The traditional *Instructions* were not, however, abandoned at once by all flag officers: in 1782, for instance, Rodney used the *Instructions*, supplemented by a large number of additional instructions, to organize his fleet at the Battle of the Saints.

In 1790 Howe issued a new signal book in which a numerary system was adopted for the admiral's signals to his fleet.[138] By this method flags had the same meaning wherever they were hoisted. There were ten basic numeral flags which read from the top down as a number, referring to a numbered signal in the book. For example, the signal for 'Prepare for Battle' was No. 53 in the book and was made by hoisting in any clearly visible position flag No. 5 (a flag quartered white and red) over No. 3 (a flag divided vertically blue/white/blue). For the repetition of a flag, to avoid the need for ships to carry several sets of signal flags, there were special 'substitute' flags. The flags were smaller than the flags used in the old *Instructions* and were designed to be easily distinct: there was only one plain dark-coloured flag, one with a diagonal cross, one vertically divided in three, one quartered, and so on, and the colours were chosen so as not to merge into one another at a distance. For signals from the individual

93 'Loss of the *Cato* and *Porpoise*, 1803', aquatint

ships to the flagship a different system was adopted, involving a different set of flags.[139]

Howe's numerary system became generally accepted and a number of variants using different flags were issued by Howe, Hood, Jervis and others in the next eight years. These books were normally issued in sets, the *Signal-Book for the Ships of War* being accompanied by *Instructions . . . explanatory of, and relative to the Signals contained in the Signal Book*, and *Night Signals*. In 1799 a more comprehensive *Signal Book for the Ships of War* was issued by the Admiralty; this standardized the signal code for the whole navy and was the first of a long series of general naval signal books. This general *Signal Book* was in use from 1799 till 1803, when it was compromised after an unofficial manuscript copy fell into the hands of the French. Accordingly, in January 1804 the numeral flags were rearranged and the book that resulted was the one in use at Trafalgar. The signal flown from the *Victory* at the beginning of the battle was No. 16, 'Engage the enemy more closely': flag No. 1 (a blue cross on a white field) over No. 6 (divided horizontally blue over white over red).

Although this system, using up to three flags in a hoist, provided a wider range of signals than the old *Instructions*, it was still limited in that only those signals could be made which were listed in the *Signal Book*. To increase its scope, particularly for two-way communication, a supplementary 'vocabulary' was devised by Captain Sir Home Popham in 1800. In Popham's system the numeral flags of the *Signal Book*, when hoisted with a special 'Telegraph Flag', referred not to signals in the *Signal Book* but to a numbered 'dictionary' of words and sentences. The numbers 1 to 25 in the vocabulary were allotted to the letters of the alphabet, and with these any word not listed in the 'dictionary' could be spelt. The first edition of Popham's *Telegraphic Signals or Marine Vocabulary* was printed in 1800; a more comprehensive version was produced in 1803, and a further much expanded edition using letters as well as numbers in 1812. This was issued to the navy in 1813, and from that time, vocabulary signals were part of the official flag signalling code of the Royal Navy.

Nelson's signal to his fleet before the beginning of the Battle of Trafalgar on 21 October 1805 read ENGLAND EXPECTS THAT EVERY MAN WILL DO HIS DUTY and was made in Popham's vocabulary, using the numeral flags of the general *Signal Book* as re-arranged in 1803. The signals officer of the *Victory* at the time was Lieutenant John Pasco, who gave, many years later, this account of the incident:

His Lordship came to me on the poop, and after ordering certain signals to be made, about a quarter to noon, he said, 'Mr Pasco, I wish to say to the fleet, "England confides that every man will do his duty"'; and he added, 'you must be quick for I have one more to make, which is for Close Action'. I replied, 'if your Lordship will permit me to substitute the "expects" for "confides", the signal will soon be completed, because the word "expects" is in the vocabulary, and "confides" must be spelt'. His Lordship replied in haste, and with seeming satisfaction, 'That will do, Pasco, make it directly'; when it had been answered by a few ships in the van, he ordered me to make the signal for Close Action and to keep it up; accordingly I hoisted No. 16 at the top-gallant mast-head and there it remained until shot away.[140]

The flags used in the signal are shown on the page opposite. The word 'duty' was not in the vocabulary and had to be spelt out. In Popham's 25-letter Alphabet I and J were treated as one letter and V preceded U; so U = 21, T = 19, and Y = 24.

In 1808 and 1816 the Admiralty revised the general *Signal Book*. In 1827 a recast series of signal books was issued, consisting of a *General Signal Book*, a *Vocabulary Signal Book* and a book of *Night and Fog Signals*. With modifications these books remained basic to British naval signalling until well into the 20th century.[141] Since the mid-19th century, flag signalling has yielded much of its importance to signalling methods based on semaphore machines and hand semaphore, flashing lamps, and eventually radio (introduced into Royal Navy ships in the early years of the 20th century). Flags currently in use in Royal Navy signalling are illustrated in the *Admiralty Manual of Seamanship*.

Merchant service codes

There existed already in the 18th-century signalling codes for the use of the ships of the East India Company, but there was no generally understood flag 'language' by which ordinary merchant ships could signal to one another, except for certain conventions such as the hoisting of the ensign

94 *Crystal Stream* (topsail schooner launched in 1877), watercolour by A de Clerk; she is making her number, QLVR, in the Commercial (International) Code

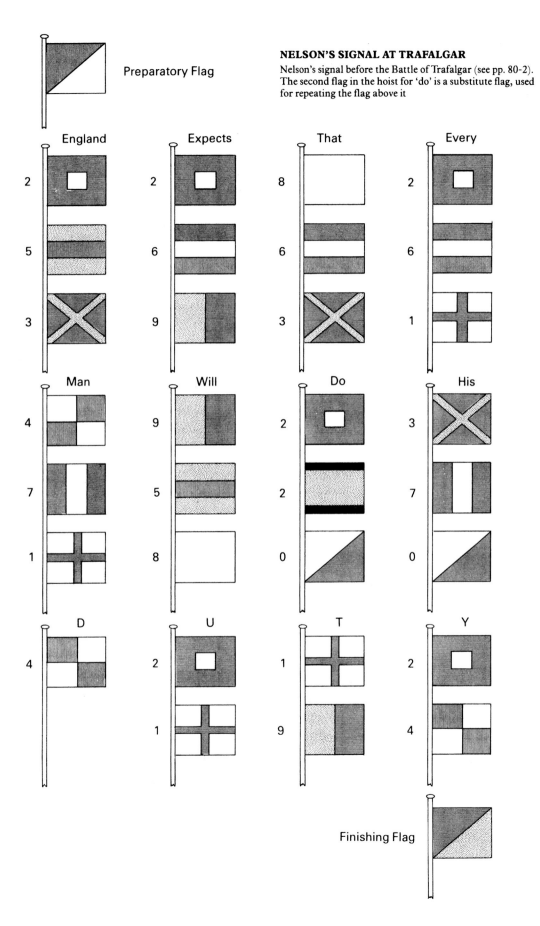

Preparatory Flag

NELSON'S SIGNAL AT TRAFALGAR
Nelson's signal before the Battle of Trafalgar (see pp. 80-2).
The second flag in the hoist for 'do' is a substitute flag, used
for repeating the flag above it

England

2
5
3

Expects

2
6
9

That

8
6
3

Every

2
6
1

Man

4
7
1

Will

9
5
8

Do

2
2
0

His

3
7
0

D

4

U

2
1

T

1
9

Y

2
4

Finishing Flag

95 A ship dressed overall, anonymous watercolour, late 18th century

upside-down as a signal of distress (Fig. 93).

This gap was successfully filled in 1817 when Captain Frederick Marryat, RN, produced his *Code of Signals for the Merchant Service*. The principle of Marryat's code, like Popham's, was numerary, with ten basic numeral flags. By hoisting groups of numeral flags beneath one of various distinguishing flags or pennants, reference could be made to the various sections of the code: names of men-of-war; names of merchantmen; names of ports, headlands, etc.; sentences; vocabulary. The book included a list of merchant ships with their individual numbers;

these became more numerous in successive editions until the later editions have to group the names of ships under four separate distinguishing pennants. Marryat's code flags are illustrated on the back endpaper. Paintings of 19th-century merchant ships sometimes show them identifying themselves by 'making their number' with a hoist from Marryat's code (Fig. 42). Although artists by no means always get it right, it is sometimes possible to identify a ship portrait by reference to an edition of Marryat's code of the right date.

Marryat's book was an international success,

going through no less than nineteen editions between 1817 and 1879 (not including foreign language editions), including a thorough revision in 1841; successive editions grew fatter and fatter as the list of merchant ships grew longer and longer. After the eighth edition in 1841 the rights were sold and later editions were produced by J.M. Richardson and later G.B. Richardson. The twelfth (1854) and subsequent editions were re-titled *Universal Code of Signals*. The preface to this twelfth edition claimed, accurately enough, that 'an European vessel is rarely met unprovided with these signals'.[142] There were, however, several rival systems in circulation in the middle of the century.

In 1857 a new code entitled the *Commercial Code of Signals* (later, from about 1870, known as the *International Code*) was published on the authority of the British Board of Trade; over the next twenty years or so this superseded Marryat, though there is evidence of Marryat being still in occasional use as late as 1890. The new code made use of several of Marryat's flags, but the principle was not numerary but alphabetical. The vowels were omitted in the early editions for a delicate reason:

The omission of the vowels was forced upon us from the circumstance, that by introducing them every objectionable word composed of four letters or less, not only in our own but in foreign languages, would appear in the Code in the course of the permutation of the letters of the Alphabet.[143]

Under the system adopted in the *Commercial/International Code* ships could 'make their number' by hoisting the group of four signal letters assigned to them; these can be found arranged as a dictionary of signal letters in the *Mercantile Navy List* from 1857 to 1864, and subsequently in the *Commercial Code List*, later the *British Code List*, later *Signal Letters of British Ships*. The *Mercantile Navy Lists* and *Lloyd's Registers* gave signal letters arranged alphabetically by ship's name. Comprehensive revisions of the

International Code were published in 1900, 1934 and 1969; a ship portrait shown making her number in the code can, if the flags are accurate, be identified by reference to a suitable edition of the code and the appropriate one of the above publications. It is not difficult to tell whether a ship in the 19th-century picture is 'making her number' in Marryat or in the *Commercial/International Code*: in Marryat the uppermost flag in such a signal will be pennant-shaped (Fig. 42), in the *Commercial Code* it is a rectangular flag (Fig. 94). The flags of the *Commercial/International Code* from 1857 to 1900 are illustrated on the page opposite.

There is a satisfying continuity in the meanings of some of the current *International Code* flags. The 'Blue Peter', a blue flag pierced white (that is, with a white rectangle in the centre) which is P in the code, has the meaning when used by itself by a ship in port, 'All persons report on board – vessel is about to proceed to sea'; it is recorded with more or less the same meaning as early as the 1750s.[144] The plain yellow flag (Q) has the meaning when used by itself 'My vessel is healthy and I request free pratique'; this meaning was established in Britain by an Act of Parliament in 1825 and its use is recorded earlier.[145]

Signal flags are also used nowadays in 'dressing ship'. The custom of putting out all available flags for a special occasion goes back at least as far as the 16th century. For example, during Francis Drake's voyage round the world, a Spanish prisoner recorded him ordering 'all the pennants and flags which the ship carried' to be put out on a Sunday on the *Golden Hind*.[146] In the 18th century national ensigns were sometimes used to dress ship, but in the 19th century it became normal to use signal flags so as to avoid the possibility of dispute over one national ensign being placed below another. Since 1889 the Royal Navy has made use of a stipulated order of flags for dressing ship, and large shipping companies have regulations of their own.[147]

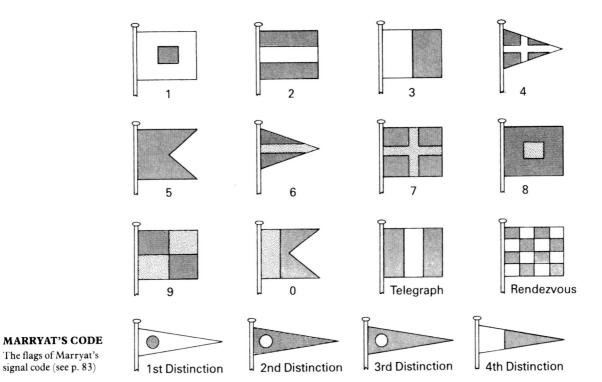

MARRYAT'S CODE

The flags of Marryat's signal code (see p. 83)

1 2 3 4

5 6 7 8

9 0 Telegraph Rendezvous

1st Distinction 2nd Distinction 3rd Distinction 4th Distinction

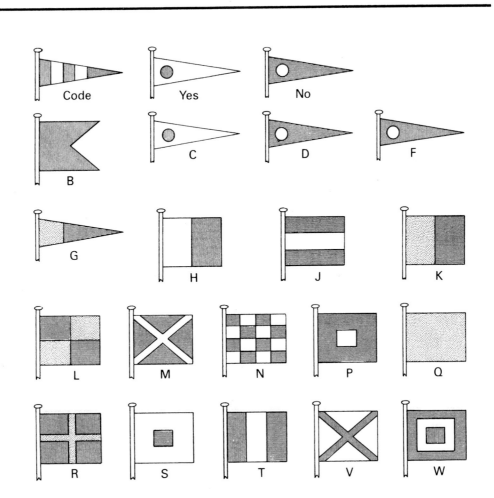

COMMERCIAL CODE

The flags of the Commercial (International) code, 1857-1900

Code Yes No

B C D F

G H J K

L M N P Q

R S T V W

CHAPTER 6

The Manufacture of Sea Flags

Materials

The care and expense lavished on the banners and streamers made for Henry VIII's navy is documented in surviving invoices (App. A). The banners and streamers supplied in 1514 for the *Henri Grace à Dieu* by John Brown and Vincenzo Volpe were the work of professional painters working with luxury materials: gold and silver leaf ('beaten gold and silver'), gold and silver thread ('wrought with gold and silver'), and silk fringes are prominent in the accounts. The cost of forty or forty-two shillings each for banners is high; the flags of St George in the same invoice, for more routine use, were priced at a mere tenpence (under a shilling) each. They would have been made of cheaper linen or woollen cloth, and were probably sewn from red and white material, rather than painted.[148]

Expenditure on a considerable scale for naval flags continued into Queen Elizabeth's reign. The ships that fought against the Spanish Armada in 1588 were fitted out with ensigns of silk or 'fine bewpers', as well as the more basic flags of St George.[149] Drake and Hawkins, when setting out in 1594 for the West Indies, provided themselves with flags, streamers and ensigns at the prodigious cost of £221; these included three streamers with the Queen's badges in silver and gold costing £8 each.[150]

In the 17th century extravagant flags of this sort continued to be made for special occasions, but the elaborate heraldic banners and streamers of the Tudor navy eventually gave way to more workaday flags. By the time of the Dutch Wars, British warships were equipped with large ensigns, jacks and command flags of relatively simple, standardized design. These were usually made of the hard-wearing woollen fabric (normally of rather loose plain tabby weave) which was known in the 17th century as 'bewpers' but which later came to be called 'bunting'. The designs were cut out of different colours of material and sewn together. Sewn 'bewpers' flags of the 1650s and 1660s survive at the National Maritime Museum and at the Rijksmuseum in Amsterdam.[151]

Linen was not often used for British naval flags, but was commonly used in navies such as the Spanish, where flags often required the painting of elaborate heraldic devices.

Flags for the Royal Navy were made both in the Royal Dockyards and by private contractors.[152] Things did not always go smoothly. A series of passages in Pepys's *Diary* between 1664 and 1666 describes the problems he had when faced with the job of organizing the supply of flags to the navy at a time when bewpers was in short supply. He coped with the difficulty by going to the markets himself and buying up a quantity of calico, which he then re-sold to the Navy. Since calico was cheaper than bewpers, Pepys congratulated himself that he was saving the King money; but he himself made a tidy profit on the deal.[153]

Painted silk flags continued to be made for royalty and for special occasions, especially where complex heraldic designs were involved. In 1677, Pepys was concerned with providing flags for the Prince and Princess of Orange (the future William and Mary) on their voyage back to Holland after their wedding: the flags were 'not made in the manner used in the navy, but painted upon crimson silk with the metals of gold and silver'.[154]

Through the 18th and 19th centuries, 100 per cent wool bunting remained the standard material for British naval flags. The successive editions from 1911 to 1937 of the *Admiralty Manual of Seamanship* noted that there was a distinction between official and other bunting: 'Each cloth of bunting (18 inches in width) has a few thicker threads worked not only into its edges but also at every 6 inches of its warp, and this mark shows the bunting to be of government make.' In 1955 the navy abandoned the traditional all-wool formula for a 75 per cent nylon, 25 per cent wool worsted. More recently 100 per cent synthetic material has been adopted – at first nylon, but when

96 The colour loft at HM Dockyard, Chatham, January 1983, shortly before 'privatisation'

this did not prove satisfactory it was replaced in 1982 by a specification for polyester.

Flag sizes

Note: Metric equivalents are approximations, measured to the nearest tenth of a metre.

The streamer supplied in 1514 for the mainmast of the *Henri Grace à Dieu*, which was 51 yards (46.6 metres) long 'and the breadth according', was one of the largest flags ever flown in the British navy. In the years that followed, masthead streamers became smaller. A later 16th-century list of 'the syzes of Streamers and Banners fitt for the Queens Ships' gives the size of the largest streamers as 9 feet (2.7 metres) at the hoist and 28 yards (25.6 metres) long; the smallest was 6 feet (1.8 metres) at the hoist and 12 yards (11.0 metres) long.[155]

Illustrations of the ships of Henry VIII's navy show them decorated at deck level with squarish banners. The numerous banners listed in the 1514 accounts are variously 3 and 3½ yards (2.7 metres and 3.2 metres) long. In Elizabeth's reign this gorgeous display of banners was restricted and the

Queen's ships normally carried a stern ensign and one or two other flags. In the 16th century these remained rather square in proportions; four flags with the Royal Arms mentioned in accounts in 1574 were 13 feet 6 inches broad and 15 feet long (4.1 by 4.6 metres).[156] Towards the end of the century, naval flags began to become more elongated: to judge from contemporary illustrations, a proportion of about 4:5 was typical in the 1590s.

In the first half of the 17th century the great streamers that had dominated ships of the Tudor navy went out of fashion, and smaller pennants came into use for squadronal distinction and for ornament. Stern ensigns, jacks, and masthead flags of command came to be the main flags of a fleet of warships; being made in simple designs, and of relatively cheap material, they grew larger. They also continued to grow proportionately longer.

The traditional way of measuring flags in the Royal Navy is 'breadths' along the hoist, a unit of measurement related to the width in which the material used to be woven. In the 17th century a breadth was about eleven inches (28cm); Pepys recorded that 'it is in general to be noted that the bewper of which Colours are made being 22 inches [56cm] in breadth and the half of that breadth or 11 inches [28cm] going in ordinary discourse by the name of a Breadth then wrought into Colours, every such breadth is allowed about half-a-yard [46cm] for its Fly'.[157] This implies an average breadth:length proportion of about 3:5 for naval flags in the second half of the 17th century.

The largest naval warships of the late 17th century flew some extremely large flags. A surviving list of flags supplied from Chatham Dockyard in 1691 includes an ensign for the flagship of 32 breadths, nearly 30 feet along the hoist by 48 feet long (9.1 by 14.6 metres).[158] A table drawn up by Pepys in 1687 laid down the following flag sizes for the different rates of ship:[159]

FIRST RATE
 ensigns and flags:
 26 breadths, 14 yards (12.8 metres) long
 jacks: 14 breadths, 7 yards (6.4 metres) long
 pennants: 3 breadths, 32 yards (29.3 metres) long

SECOND RATE
 ensigns and flags:
 22 breadths, 12½ yards (11.4 metres) long
 jacks: 12 breadths, 6 yards (5.5 metres) long
 pennants: 3 breadths, 29 yards (26.5 metres) long

THIRD RATE
 ensigns and flags:
 20 breadths, 11 yards (10.1 metres) long
 jacks: 10 breadths, 5 yards (4.6 metres) long
 pennants: 3 breadths, 28 yards (25.6 metres) long

FOURTH RATE
 ensigns and flags:
 18 breadths, 10 yards (9.1 metres) long
 jacks: 10 breadths, 5 yards (4.6 metres) long
 pennants: 3 breadths, 24 yards (21.9 metres) long

FIFTH RATE
 ensigns and flags:
 16 breadths, 8 yards (7.3 metres) long
 jacks: 8 breadths, 4 yards (3.7 metres) long
 pennants: 3 breadths, 22 yards (20.1 metres) long

It is to be noticed that the jacks are squarer in proportion, as well as much smaller, than the ensigns and command flags.

Of surviving 17th-century British flags, the Commonwealth flag at Greenwich (Plate XI) measures approximately 15 feet by 20 feet (4.6 by 6.2 metres); one of the red ensigns at the Rijksmuseum is approximately 9 feet 6 inches by 14 feet (2.9 by 4.3 metres).[160]

Flags remained very large through the 18th century, although by the Napoleonic Wars, admirals' flags were considerably smaller and rather squarer than ensigns. A white ensign supposed to have been used by the *Brunswick* at the Battle of the 'Glorious First of June', 1794, measures 20 feet by 40 feet (6.1 by 12.2 metres); the Union Flag flown by Lord Howe in the *Queen Charlotte* as his flag of command at the same battle (Plate VII) is a relatively modest 12 feet by 17 feet (3.7 by 5.2 metres).

By the beginning of the 19th century, a 'breadth' had shrunk and reached its modern meaning of 9 inches (23cm) along the hoist. An 'Establishment of English Colours for ships', approved for Chatham Dockyard in 1822 gives the following flag sizes for the various rates of warships:[161]

FIRST RATE
 ensigns of 26, 16 and 10 breadths
 jacks of 10 breadths
 pennants 24 yards (21.9 metres) long

THIRD RATE
 ensigns of 23, 15 and 10 breadths
 jacks of 10 breadths
 pennants 24 yards (21.9 metres) long

FOURTH RATE
 (Leander's class)
 ensigns of 22, 15 and 10 breadths
 jacks of 9 breadths
 pennants 22 yards (20.1 metres) long

FOURTH RATE
 (2-decker)
 ensigns of 22, 14 and 10 breadths
 jacks of 8 breadths
 pennants 22 yards (20.1 metres) long

FIFTH RATE
 (50-42 guns)
 ensigns of 20, 14 and 10 breadths
 jacks of 8 breadths
 pennants of 20 yards (18.3 metres) long

FIFTH RATE

(34-32 guns)

ensigns of 16, 12 and 8 breadths

jacks of 8 breadths

pennants 18 yards (16.5 metres) long

SIXTH RATE

ensigns of 14, 10 and 8 breadths

jacks of 6 breadths

pennants 16 yards (14.6 metres) long

These flags are rather smaller than 18th-century ones. An ensign of 26 breadths was rather less than 20 feet by 40 feet (6.1 by 12.2 metres); in 1742 the largest naval ensigns had been about 28 feet by 51 feet (8.5 by 15.5 metres).

Under Queen Victoria flags shrank further, and proportions were standardized. Ensigns and jacks were to be made in a proportion of 1:2, admirals' flags in a proportion of 2:3. 'Whip' pennants are usually four inches (10cm) at the hoist. The regulation sizes for naval flags are laid down in the official publication *Flags of All Nations*.

The measurement of flags in breadths is peculiar to the Royal Navy. Flag makers usually measure flags in yards of length; thus a flag 6 feet by 12 feet (1.8 by 3.7 metres) is called in the navy a flag of 8 breadths, but elsewhere a flag of four yards. Merchant shipping house flags are not covered by official dictates: they are most commonly made in a proportion of 2:3

In the 17th century signal flags, when they were not simply the regular command flags and ensigns hoisted in particular parts of the ship, were the same size as them. This remained true during the supremacy of the *Fighting Instructions*. The numerary codes introduced at the end of the 18th century meant that three or four signal flags might have to be hoisted at a single masthead, and they became smaller. A Navy Board letter of 1790 listing signal flags 'to be used by Lord Howe' states that on the larger ships they are to be '14 breadths, or about 12 ft broad, 14 ft long' (3.7 by 4.3 metres) and on the smaller 'about 10 ft broad, 12 ft long' (3.0 and 3.7 metres).[162]

As for merchant service signals, Marryat's code

suggested 6 feet by 8 feet (1.8 by 2.4 metres) as the size for the largest signal flags, with 4 feet by 18 feet (1.2 by 5.5 metres) for the corresponding pennants. The most common sizes for the signal flags of the *International Code* nowadays are (a) 6 feet 6 inches by 8 feet (2.0 by 2.4 metres) (b) 4 feet 6 inches by 5 feet 6 inches (1.4 by 1.7 metres) (c) 2 feet 6 inches by 3 feet (0.8 by 0.9 metres).

Flag fixings

In the 16th century, heraldic banners and ensigns were as a rule fastened to their flagstaffs or provided with sockets that slipped over the staffs. Tudor banners were sometimes 'amphibious': when required for land service the flagstaffs could be unshipped and carried ashore.

The system for streamers was quite different. The streamer had a rod at the hoist with a rope attached to either end; this rope was attached to a fixing in the tops. A similar method became normal for the pennants of 17th- and 18th-century warships.

Early in the 17th century, as sea flags grew larger and more distinct from the flags used on land, it became normal for them to be attached to the staff all along the hoist, with rings or loops or a continuous lacing. This was not a method which made for rapid hoisting or lowering of flags, especially in the tops, and gradually it came to be superseded by the modern system of halyards: a rope is sewn through the hoist of the flag and this can be attached at either end to a halyard which passes through a block at the top of the flagstaff or mast; the flag is raised or lowered by pulling the halyard. This system was in use before the end of the 17th century, but did not totally supersede the older system until the end of the 18th.[163]

The most common method of attaching the flag to the halyard nowadays is for the flag to be fitted with a double-ended wooden peg called a toggle at the head of the hoist, and an eye or loop at the tail end. These marry up with a corresponding eye and toggle on the halyard. Since the turn of the century the Royal Navy has instead used 'Inglefield clips', interlocking metal swivel clips which engage with others on hoist and halyard; these are not widely used in the merchant service, although some shipping companies have adopted them.

CHAPTER 7

The Flag Collection at the National Maritime Museum

The flags at the National Maritime Museum, which number nearly 800, have been brought together from various sources. Many have come into the collection by gift or bequest, others have been transferred from the Admiralty, the Greenwich Hospital Collection, and the Royal United Services Museum, which was dispersed in 1963. A number of flags have been lent to the Museum, among them some important relics of 18th-century naval battles which have remained in the possession of descendants of men who took part.

The most numerous group is the reference collection of shipping company house flags. Most of these come from two large collections – one made by C.M. Pope, the other begun by D.R. Bolt and the property of the London Borough of Tower Hamlets, which has deposited them on loan at Greenwich.[164] The Museum hopes to make the collection of house flags as comprehensive as possible.

Much of the rest of the collection consists of British maritime, and particularly naval, relics and trophies. These range in date from the cross and harp standard (see above p.19 and Plate XI), which was probably made about 1652-4, to the Royal Standard and anchor flag flown by the Royal Yacht *Britannia* during Queen Elizabeth II's Silver Jubilee tour of the Commonwealth in 1977. Several of the flags at the Museum reflect the history of the Royal Navy in the 'age of Nelson': these include the Union Flag flown at the main by Lord Howe in his flagship the *Queen Charlotte* at the battle of the 'Glorious First of June', 1794 (Plate VII), and a white ensign said to have been worn by the *Brunswick* at the same battle;[165] the blue command flag used by Duncan at the Battle of Camperdown, 1797; and several pieces of the *Victory's* white ensign at Trafalgar: this was carried in procession at Nelson's funeral at St Paul's Cathedral and, at the end of the service, 'the honest tars who bore into the church the ensign of the *Victory*, desirous of retaining some mementoes of their great and favourite commander, tore off a considerable part of the largest flag, of which most, if not all, of

them obtained a small portion; though few other persons were able to get any'.[166] Also in the collection are British naval flags from the Crimean and Boer Wars and both the World Wars of the 20th century.

Naval flags are often preserved by being captured and valued as trophies, and at the Museum is a varied collection of foreign flags taken in naval actions since the middle of the 18th century. Spanish examples include a much patched linen flag taken from the Morro Castle when Havana was captured in 1762 (Fig. 97) and a huge ensign some 49 by 33 feet (about 15 by 10 metres), worn by the *San Ildefonso* at Trafalgar and afterwards displayed at Nelson's funeral. The most evocative of the French flags captured during the Revolutionary and Napoleonic Wars is a banner embroidered with the words: MARINS LA REPUBLIQUE OU LA MORT from *L'Amérique* at the battle of the 'Glorious First of June' (Fig. 98); there is also a tricolour taken at Trafalgar. Three Dutch flags from the period of the 'Batavian Republic' (1795-1806) have painted linen cantons with the Republic's device of Liberty with the 'Cap of Liberty' and a lion (Plate XIII; Fig. 81). The most notable United States flag is the fragmentary 15-star 'Stars and Stripes' from the American frigate *Chesapeake* captured in her battle with the British *Shannon* in 1813 (Fig. 68). German flags of the 20th century include one used in the First World War by the Kaiser (Fig. 103) and one used in the Second by the Chief of the Nazi navy Grossadmiral Dönitz (Fig. 104). From Russia there are early Revolutionary flags (Fig. 102) as well as Crimean War trophies.

Among the most attractive flags in the collection are a group which record the imperialist role of the Royal Navy in the 19th century. These include some beautiful Chinese silk flags with painted or embroidered decoration, which were taken during naval operations in the Far East around the middle of the century (back cover). The flags taken during the Benin (Nigeria) campaigns of 1894 and 1897, by contrast, have a comically macabre quality (Fig. 100).

97 *(left)* Fragments of a much-patched Spanish flag from the Morro Castle, Havana, 1762; on loan from the Earl of Albemarle; the main piece approx 270 × 300 cm

98 *(below, left)* Flag of the boarding division of *L'Amérique*, taken at the Battle of the First of June 1794. 65 × 65 cm

99 *(below, right)* French Royalist flag, said to have been used on HMS *Hebrus* c 1815. 280 × 390 cm

100 Flag captured by the British expedition against Benin, West Africa, in 1897. 170 × 348 cm

90

101 White ensign used on HMS *Iron Duke*, Jellicoe's flagship at the Battle of Jutland, 1916. 152 × 305 cm

102 *(left)* Russian revolutionary flag, c 1919. The initials stand for 'Russian Soviet Federal Socialist Republic'. 109 × 162 cm

103 *(below, left)* Flag of German Grossadmiral, used by the Kaiser during World War I. 97 × 102 cm

104 *(below, right)* Flag of German Grossadmiral during World War II. 150 × 150 cm

There are other flags in the Museum less closely associated with naval history: particularly splendid is the group of Royal Standards of the late 18th and 19th centuries, some of them of painted silk (Plate XII). Also worth mentioning, and typical of the variety of the collection, are the racing flag of the yacht *Britannia*, which belonged to Edward VII (Fig. 59); some large triangular prize pennants of sailing barges victorious in Thames and Medway barge races; and several flags from voyages of polar exploration.

Few of these flags are on permanent display at Greenwich – mainly because of their size – but they can be seen by appointment.

The National Maritime Museum collection is the most important collection of historic British sea flags, but it is not the only place where such flags can be seen. Eight flags traditionally said to have been used by Sir Francis Drake are at Buckland Abbey in Devon; the Rijksmuseum in Amsterdam contains a number of English sea flags captured during the 'Dutch Wars'; and there is a large collection of more modern naval flags at the Imperial War Museum. The staff of the National Maritime Museum are always interested to learn of historic sea flags in private collections.

105 Samuel Pepys (1633-1703) – the first English 'vexillologist'?
Oil painting by Kneller

APPENDIX A

Accounts for flags supplied to the *Henri Grace à Dieu*, 1514

1(a) British Library, Stowe MS.146, fol. 112-113.

Memorandum this parcells here after foloyng maed by me John Brown the kynges peyntor for the kynges Royall Shipp callid the henrie grace a diew the xth day of aprill the vth yere of the reigne of our lord kyng henre the viii[th]

In primus a large stremer for the mayn mast conteinyng li yerdis long and the bredith a cordyng and frengid with cadas freng for shapyng sowyng and workmanship of this same stremer the price iii li (iii li vi s viii d)

item x baners of tewke betyn gold and sillver and frengid with silke every of them ii yerdes di long and the bredith acordyng affter the raet for stoof and workmanship price of a pece xlii s : xxi li

this parcells herafter foloyng maed and delyverd to Thomas Spert master of the henre grace a diew by the kynges commandment for the kynges gret boot

Item a stremer in length xx yerdes and the bredith acordyng for Shapyng sowyng and wormanship of this stremer the price xx s (xxiii s iiii d)

Item allso x baners of tewk wroght with golld and silver and frengid with silke every them iii yerdis long and the bredith acordyng for stuff and work-manship price apece xl s ; xx li

Item for ii flagges with crossis of Seyntt Georg for shapyng sowyng and for freng price of a pece x d. Summa xxd

Item viii flagis with crossis of Seint George price a pece x d. Summa vi s viii d . . .

. . . Memorandum maed by William heyward Joiner lx stavises for the Kynges grett Shipp price of a pece xvi d. Summa iiii li

Item for payntyng of the Seyd Stavis in the Kynges coluris in oyle price of a pece vi d (viii d) Summa xxx s (xl s). . .

. . . Receyved by me John browne of London paynter of Sir John Daunce by the kynges comaundement: Four score thyrtene poundes two shillinges and eight pens sterling for the parcelles afore conteyned in thys boke In witnesse wherof I the said John browne to thys presentes have subscrybed my marke and sett my sealle the xxvi day of aprill anno sexto Regis henricum VIII[m]

1(b) BL, Stowe MS. 146, fol. 114

Received of John Broune paynter un to our sovereyn lord kyng harry the viii

    En primus a baner of ynglond and Spayne

    Item a baner of Castyll

    Item a baner of Wallyes

    Item a baner with the povindegarnett [pome-granate] and the Rosse

    Item a baner of Inglond

    Item a baner of Cornwall

    Item a baner with a Rosse of wyght and grene

    Item a baner of Ynglond

    Item a baner of Gyan [Guienne]

    Item a baner of Sent Edward

By me Thomas Spertt master of the Henre Grosse dew

2 BL, Stowe MS. 146, fol. 124

Thise be the parcelles of stremers and baners whiche Vinsent Vulp peyntoure by the commaundment of the kinges noble grace hath peynted and made for his newe ship

First a stremer with a dragon conteynyng in lenght xlv yerdes and brede according to the same lenght for frenge and workemanship iii li

Item a stremer with a dragon conteynyng in lenght xlii yerdes and brede according for frenge and workemanship xl s (liii s iiii d)

Item a stremer with a lyon conteynyng in lenght xxxvi yerdes and brede according for frenge and workemanship xxvi s viii d (xl s)

Item a stremer with a grehound conteynyng in lenght xviii yerdes and brede according for frenge and workemanship xv s (xxv s)

Item ii litell Stremers with crosse of saint George conteynyng in lenght the one xv yerdes and the other xii yerdes and brede according for frenge and workemanship xviii s

Item a C of penselles xii d (xvi ; viii) the pece. Summa Cs (vi li xiii s iiii d ; lxvi s viii d)

Item fyfty baners of tuke wrought with gold and silver for stuf frenge and workemanship xl s (xlii s) a pece Summa C li (Cv li)

Summa totalis Cxii li xix s viii d (Cxxi li ix s viii d)

Receyved by me Vincent Fox of Sir John Daunce knighte the ii^d day of Juyne anno vi^to Regis h viii° by his commaundment the somme of one hunderth twelve poundes nynetene shillinges and eight pennce sterling for the parcelles within wryten delyverd to the Kinges Shippe called the henry grace de due In wittness wherof I the said Vincent Fox to this bille have subscribed my Name the day and yere abovesaid

Io Vincenzo Volpe son contento di quanto ho lavorato per la carraca come sono bander et stremer

Note: Figures in brackets in these accounts are figures deleted in the manuscript. There were evidently disputes about the price.

Extracts from Nathaniel Boteler's discussion of flags in

Dialogues about Sea Services (written *c.* 1634; reprinted from the Navy Records Society edition, 1929)

Admiral:

And yet we must hear somewhat more of this subject; about the carrying out of flags and the like.

Captain:

Flags (to speak properly), are only those which are borne out in the tops of ships; and they serve as badges, and that as well for the distinguishing of nations as Commanders. And thus the Admiral of a Fleet or any Squadron is known to be so, by his ship's carrying of her flag in her main top; the Vice-Admiral by having his in the fore top, and the Rear-Admiral his in the mizen top. And of what nation they are is known either by the crosses that they have in their flags, or the colours of the nation or country they are of. As St George's cross (as it is called) of old for England, and of late, the British flag; St Andrew's Cross for Scotland; the French white cross for France; and so for Denmark and the rest. And the Commonwealths and States (finding no room to distinguish themselves by crosses, being all taken up by the monarchs) do it either by the distinction of colours; as the United Provinces by their blue and white, or by some device or portraiture that they carry in their flags, as the Venetians by their St Mark. And thus far it is usual and useful even with fleets of merchantmen who agree among themselves, for the Admiral ships in this kind. But in a royal fleet, consisting mainly of men-of-war, wheresoever the Prince is there in person, or his High Admiral in his room, there is then carried out in the main top of the ship, where they go in person, in lieu of ordinary flags, the Standard Royal, that is the arms and escutcheon of the Kingdom of which they are.

Admiral:

Is this Standard Royal to be carried out only by the Prince or his High Admiral in their proper persons?

Captain:

I once (and only once) saw it carried abroad by a mere General or Admiral of the Fleet for a whole voyage together; but (as I take it) it was granted unto him rather as favour than a right.

Admiral:

What are the respects and dues belonging unto these flags when they are seen thus flying abroad?

Captain:

It is requirable that all ships and fleets, being inferiors either in respect of sovereignty, or place, or part, or any the like relations, do express an acknowledgement and submission by taking in of their own flags, whensoever they meet with any others that are (justly) their superiors in any of these respects. As in the point of sovereignty within our Narrow Seas and English channels, which have long been claimed and made good to be a right, appertaining to the monarchs of England; if any fleet whatsoever shall, in any of these parts, meet with any Admiral serving in his Majesty's pay, and especially if it be any one of his Majesty's own ships, and giving notice of herself by having her flag flying, and if this fleet shall not submit to this submission and acknowledgement by taking in all their flags in their tops, it is to be accounted such an affront as that, upon terms of obstinacy, they are to be treated as enemies. In brief, no stranger of what condition soever ought to open his flag in any port of England, or in any place within any of his Majesty's dominions where there is any ship of his Majesty's own, or in his service, upon the penalty (at the least, and that upon submission) of losing her flag and to pay for the expense in powder that shall be spent in compelling thereunto. And all English ships themselves, unless in his Majesty's service, incur the same penalty upon the same misdemeanour. . .

Admiral:

... But what other flags have you at sea, and what are their use and expressions?

Captain:

In strictness of terms, as I said before, those only which are carried out of the tops are to be called Flags; the other are named either Colours, Ensigns, or Pendants.

Admiral:

Colours and Ensigns I take to be all one, but where are they to be placed, and wherefore serve they?

Captain:

They are placed in the sterns or poops of ships; and few ships there are, whether men-of-war or merchantmen, that are without them. And their service is, that when any strange ships meet one with another at sea, or find one another in any harbour or road, by the showing abroad these Ensigns or Colours, it is known one to another of what country they are, and to what place they belong.

Admiral:

Serve the Colours or Ensigns for no other employments, but only this?

Captain:

Yes, to many other, by way of direction; as shall be set down largely in our next day's discourse.

Admiral:

What are the Pendants you mentioned even now, and wherefore serve they?

Captain:

A Pendant is a long piece [of silk] or some other stuff, cut out pointed-wise towards the end, in form of a streamer; where they are slit into two parts. And the use of them is to distinguish the Squadrons of great fleets, by hanging them out in the tops of such ships as carry no flags. As for example, all such ships as are of the Admiral's Squadron, are to hang them out in their main tops; those of the Vice-Admiral's Squadron, in their fore tops; and those of the Rear Admiral's in their mizen tops; and here also they are to be of several colours. But besides this use, in great ships, and especially such as belong to the King, they are often used by way of trim and bravery; and are then hung out at every yard arm, and at the heads of the masts. And these only are their uses, and employments. And these also the only colours, pendants and flags anciently carried abroad and used in ships of war. But of late there hath been invented an order that none of our English ships should be allowed to carry the King's flag, (that is, the English cross quartered with the Scottish and called the British flag or colours) save only such ships as are either of his Majesty's own or serve under his pay. And every such vessel, though but a catch [ketch] is permitted and enjoined to wear one of these in a small volume in her bolt-sprit's top. And these flags, thus worn, are termed jacks.

A Proclamation Concerning Colours to be Worn on Board Ships, 1694.

Whereas divers of Their Majesties Subjects have of late presumed on Board their Ships to wear Their Majesties Jacks, Pendants and Ensigns, which according to Ancient Usage have been appointed as a distinction for Their Majesties Ships, and many times thinking to evade the punishment due for the same, have worn Jacks, Pendants and Ensigns in shape and mixture of Colours so little different from those of Their Majesties, as not without difficulty to be distinguished therefrom, which practice is found attended with manifold Inconveniences: For prevention of the same for the future, Their Majesties have thought fit, with the Advice of Their Privy Council, by this Their Royal Proclamation, strictly to Charge and Command all Their Subjects whatsoever, That they do not presume to wear in any of their Ships or Vessels, Their Majesties Jack, commonly called the Union Jack, nor any Pendants, nor any such Ensigns or Colours as are usually born by Their Majesties Ships, without particular Warrant for their so doing from Their Majesties, or the Lord High Admiral of England, or the Commissioners for executing the Office of Lord High Admiral for the time being. And Their Majesties do hereby also further Command all Their Loving Subjects, that without such Warrant as aforesaid, they presume not to wear on Board their Ships or Vessels, any Jacks, Pendants, Ensigns or Colours, made in imitation of those of Their Majesties, or any other Flags, Jacks, Pendants, or Ensigns whatsoever, than those usually worn in Merchants Ships, Viz. The Flag and Jack White, with a Red Cross, commonly called St George's Cross, passing quite through the same, and the Ensign Red, with the like Cross in a Canton White at the upper Corner thereof next the Staff, nor any kind of Pendant whatsoever, saving that for the better Distinction of such Ships as shall have Commissions of Letters of Mart or Reprisals against the Enemy, and any other Ships or Vessels which may be employed by the Principal Officers and Commissioners of Their Majesties Navy, the Principal Officers of Their Majesties Ordnance, the Commissioners for Victualling Their Majesties Navy, the Commissioners for Their Majesties Customs, and the Commissioners for Transportation for Their Majesties Services, relating particularly to those Offices, Their Majesties do Command that all such ships as have Commissions of Letters of Mart or Reprisals, shall besides the Colours which may be worn by Merchants Ships, wear a Red Jack, with the Union Jack, described in a Canton at the upper Corner thereof next the staff; And that such Ships and Vessels as shall be employed for Their Majesties Service, by the Principal Officers and Commissioners of Their Majesties Navy, the Principal Officers of Their Majesties Ordnance, the Commissioners for Victualling Their Majesties Navy, the Commissioners for Their Majesties Customs, and the Commissioners for Transportation for Their Majesties Services, relating particularly to those Offices, shall wear a Red Jack with the Union Jack in a Canton at the upper Corner thereof next the Staff, as aforesaid, and in the other part of the said Jack shall be described the Seal used in the respect-Offices aforesaid, by which the said Ships and Vessels shall be employed. And Their Majesties do strictly Charge and Command, That none of Their Loving Subjects do presume to wear any of the said Distinction Jacks, unless they shall have Commissions of Letters of Mart or Reprisals, or be employed in Their Majesties Service by the before mentioned Offices respectively. And Their Majesties do hereby require the Principal Officers and Commissioners of Their Majesties Navy, The Governours of Their Forts and Castles, the Officers of Their Customs, and the Commanders or Officers of any of Their Majesties Ships, upon their meeting with, or otherwise observing any Ships or Vessels of Their Majesties Subjects, wearing any Flag, Pendant, Jack or Ensign contrary hereunto, whether at Sea or in Port, not only to Seize, or cause such Flag, Pendant, Jack or Ensign to be forthwith Seized, but also to Return the Names of the said Ships, and Vessels, together with the Names of their respective Masters or Commanders, unto the Lord High Admiral, Commissioners for executing the Office of Lord High Admiral, or the Judge of the High Court of Admiralty for the time being, to the end that the Persons offending may be duly punished for the same . . .

Given at Our Court at Whitehall, the Twelfth Day of July, 1694. In the Sixth Year of Our Reign.

'Of Colours' from the first edition of *Regulations and Instructions relating to His Majesty's Service at Sea* (1731)

Article I

Flag-Officers, and Captains, are strictly forbidden to wear any other Flag or Pendant, than what belongs to their proper Rank, except when His Majesty, or any of the Royal Family, are on board.

Article II

If any Officer, wearing a Flag or broad Pendant, shall happen to be slain in Fight with the Enemy, the said Flag or Pendant shall nevertheless continue flying, and not be taken in whilst the Enemy is in Sight; but the Admiral, who commands in Chief, as also the Flag Officer, to whose Squadron or Division he belonged, shall immediately be acquainted with it; and if it be the Commander in Chief who is killed, the next commanding Officer is to be forthwith informed of it, who shall immediately repair on board the Ship of the deceased Commander, and give the necessary Orders, leaving his own Flag or broad Pendant flying in his own Ship.

Article III

For the better Distinction of Flag-Officers passing in their Boats, the following Regulation is to be observed; the Admiral of the Fleet, the Admirals of the White and Blue, and the Vice-Admiral of the Red, may carry their proper Flags at the Head of their Boats, when they think proper; but there shall be in the other Flags the following Distinction, viz. a white Ball in the Flag of the Rear-Admiral of the Red, a blue Ball in the Flag of the Vice of the White; and two blue Balls in the Flag of the Rear of the White; a white Ball in the Flag of the Vice of the Blue, and two white Balls in the Flag of the Rear of the Blue; the said Balls to be in a Canton, at the upper Corner of the Flag, next the Staff.

Article IV

Merchant-Ships are to wear a Red Ensign, with the Union Jack in a Canton at the upper End next the Staff; and a white Jack, with a red Cross, commonly called St George's Cross, passing quite through the same.

Article V

Ships having private Commissions, or Letters of Mart or Reprizals, are to wear the same Ensign as Merchant Ships; and a Red Jack, with the Union Jack in a Canton, at the upper Corner next the Staff.

Article VI

Ships or Vessels in the Service of any publick Office, are to wear the same Ensign and Jack as Ships having Letters of Mart, only that in the Body of the Jack or Ensign, shall be likewise described the Seal of the Office they belong to.

Article VII

His Majesty strictly forbids all Masters of Merchant-Ships, as also of all Ships or Vessels employed in the Service of any publick Office, or in raising Seamen, to wear Pendants, or what may be taken for them: And if any shall presume to offend herein, and wear Flags, Pendants, or other Colours, contrary to what is here allowed, it is His Majesty's Pleasure, that the Captains, or any other Officers of His Ships of War, do seize the said Colours, and return the Names of the Master and Ship to the Secretary of the Admiralty, together with Affidavits of the Fact by two Witnesses, in order to their being proceeded against in the High Court of Admiralty.

Article VIII

The Commanders of His Majesty's Ships are not to suffer any Foreign Ships to ride in any of His Ports or Roads with False Colours; and if they persist therein after being admonished, they are to put the said Ships under Arrest, and send an Account thereof to the Secretary of the Admiralty.

APPENDIX E

Order in Council of 9 July 1864, abolishing the use of squadronal colours in the Royal Navy *(Admiralty Orders in Council*, **II (1904),** pp. 46-7)

Under the Regulations established by Your Majesty's Order in Council of the 25th day of July 1861, for the governance of the Royal Naval Service, the Flag Officers of the Fleet, whether Admirals, Vice-Admirals, or Rear-Admirals, are classed in Squadrons of the Red, White, and Blue, and are (with the exception of the Admiral of the Fleet) authorized to fly their flags of the colour of the Squadron to which they belong, this regulation necessitating the adoption of ensigns and pendants of a corresponding colour in every ship and vessel employed under their orders, each vessel is therefore supplied with three sets of colours, and the frequent alterations that have to be made when the Fleet is distributed as at present, under the Orders of many Flag Officers, is attended with much inconvenience from the uncertainty and expense which the system entails.

The increased number and size of merchant steam-ships render it a matter of importance to distinguish on all occasions men-of-war from private ships by a distinctive flag; the latter vessels bearing at present the same red ensign as your Majesty's ships when employed under an Admiral of the Red Squadron. It also appears to us to be desirable to grant (under such conditions as we may from time to time impose) the use of a distinguishing flag to such ships of the merchant service as may be employed in the public service, or whose commanding officer (with a given portion of the crew) may belong to the Royal Naval Reserve. We therefore most humbly submit that Your Majesty may be pleased by your

Order in Council to prescribe the discontinuance of the division of Flag Officers into the Red, White, and Blue Squadrons, and to order and direct that the White Ensign, with its broad and narrow pendants, be henceforward established and recognized as the colours of the Royal Naval Service, reserving the use of the Red and Blue colours for such special occasions as may appear to us or to officers in command of Fleets and Squadrons to require their adoption: the White flag with a Red St. George's Cross to be borne by Admirals, Vice-Admirals, and Rear-Admirals on their respective masts: Commodores of the first class to carry a White broad pendant with the Red Cross at the main-top-gallant-mast-head, Commodores of the second class a similar broad pendant at the fore-top-gallant-mast-head, and senior officers when two or more vessels are present to bear the broad pennant at the mizen-top-gallant-mast-head. The blue Ensign and Union Jack, with a White border, to be carried by all vessels employed in the service of any public office; by vessels employed under the Transport Department, and the Civil Departments of the Navy (with the Seal or Badge of the office to which they belong as at present), and, under our permission, by ships commanded by Officers of the Royal Naval Reserve Force, and fulfilling in other respects the conditions required to entitle them to the privilege. The Red Ensign and Union Jack, with a White border, continuing as at present the national colours for all British ships, with such exceptions in favour of Yachts and other vessels as we may from time to time authorize to bear distinguishing flags.

Notes

1 Pepys MS. 2877, pp. 375-7, contains some interesting notes made by Pepys on the different functions of sea flags; see Wilson (Bibl. B36).

2 See Oppenheim (Bibl. F15), p. 62. On Vincenzo Volpe, see E. Auerbach, 'Vincenzo Volpe, the King's Painter', *Burlington Magazine* 92 (1950), pp. 222-7. Generally, compare Perrin (Bibl. C23), pp. 43-5. The bill included a number of flags supplied for other ships.

3 For the date at which the king of England followed the example of the French king and reduced the number of lilies from many ('France Ancient') to three ('France Modern'), see M. G. Heenan, 'The French quartering in the arms of Henry VI', *Coat of Arms* 10 (1968-9), pp. 215-21. On royal and other badges, see A. C. Fox-Davies, *Heraldic Badges*, London & New York 1907. A spectacular series of illustrations of 15th century armorial streamers is in BL, Cotton MS. Julius E IV; see William Earl of Carysfort, *The Pageants of Richard Beauchamp Earl of Warwick*, Roxburghe Club 1908, especially p. xiii.

4 For the original painting, see O. Millar, *The Tudor, Stuart and Early Georgian Pictures in the Collection of H.M. the Queen*, London 1963, cat. No. 24. Compare the drawing reproduced as the frontispiece to Perrin (Bibl. C23), from BL Cotton MS. Augustus I. ii, fol. 57a. The streamers in the drawings of Henry VIII's ships towards the end of his reign in the Anthony Anthony Roll (Pepys MS. 2991 and BL Add. MS. 22047), which is an incomparable source for the flags of Henry VIII's navy, have St George's cross at the hoist, and the fly divided green and white (Plate I, no. 22). Illustrations of Tudor streamers sometimes show them split at the fly, sometimes with the end pointed. On the flags portrayed in the Anthony Anthony Roll, see Bellew (Bibl. C5).

5 H. Szymanski, 'The History of decorated and coloured sails', *MM* 13 (1927), pp. 160-6. Compare National Maritime Museum, *Impressions of Seals, etc.*, by H. H. Brindley, London 1938; and the Beauchamp Pageants (see note 3).

6 Brown's accounts for the *Henri Grace à Dieu* (App. A) include a banner with the arms of Edward the Confessor, for which see Perrin (Bibl. C23), Pl. I, no. 6, and pp. 43-5.

7 On the Reformation assault on the cult of saints, see J. Phillips, *The Reformation of Images*, Berkeley and Los Angeles 1973. There are no flags with pictures of saints on them in the Anthony Anthony Roll; some of the deck level banners are striped – forerunners of the ensigns of Elizabethan and Jacobean ships.

8 Extreme puritans took offence at the use of St George's cross in flags; see p. 47, Sergeant John Knight, who wrote an essay on the flag of St George in 1673 for Samuel Pepys (Pepys MS. 2877, pp. 402-36) regarded the 'confinement' of the cross of St George to a small canton in ensigns as a vile Puritan plot.

9 The painting was described to the Society of Antiquaries in 1773; *Archaeologia* 3, pp. 261-7.

10 Corbett (Bibl. C8), p. 16.

11 Corbett (Bibl. C8), pp. 23-4; Perrin (Bibl. C23), p. 87. These orders were a revision of orders issued a few days previously; see Corbett (Bibl. C8), p. 19.

12 Corbett (Bibl. C9), pp. 347-8.

13 Viscount Dillon, 'The Tudor Battle Flag', *Archaeological Journal* 65 (1908), pp. 282-6; H. Lumpkin, 'The Pictures of Henry VIII's Army in Cotton MS. Augustus iii', *Journal of the Arms and Armour Society* 3 (1960), p. 163. What look like 'amphibious' flags are shown in plans of Drake's attack on Spanish settlements in the West Indies in 1585-6; British Library (Bibl. F4), nos. 114, 116, 117, 118, 119; and see above, Fig. 5. See also the documents quoted by Perrin (Bibl. C23), pp. 45-6, 48.

14 An Elizabethan striped ensign with a cross of St George throughout the flag is shown in Bodleian Lib., Rawlinson MS. A 192, fol. 120. Diagonally and horizontally striped ensigns without a cross of St George are illustrated in a plan of Yarmouth made *c.* 1585: S. Tyacke and J. Huddy, *Christopher Saxton and Tudor Map-making*, British Library 1980, no. 16. Numerous other patterns of striped ensign are illustrated in various drawings and engravings of Elizabethan and Jacobean ships: see, for instance, the yellow and red striped ensign, and the streamers with St George's cross at the hoist and the fly red, in BL Cotton MS. Augustus I. i. 14. The colours of striped ensigns may on occasion have corresponded to the livery colours of the owner or captain of a ship.

15 J. K. Laughton, *The Defeat of the Spanish Armada* II, NRS 2, 1894, pp. 242-9.

16 Pepys's miscellaneous notes on flags include a memo to research the 'ancient practice of the Lord Admiral (and private Captains, I think.....) theyr wearing flags with their paternal arms...'; Pepys MS. 2877, p. 378.

17 D. W. Waters and G. P. B. Naish, *The Elizabethan Navy and the Armada of Spain*, NMM Monograph 17, 1975, p. 87.

18 Less fanciful, perhaps, than most is the illustration of the *Ark Royal* in Plate 22 of the first English edition, published in 1588, of the Dutch sea atlas, the *Mariner's Mirror;* the ship is shown with a flag of the royal arms on a striped field at the main. Compare the woodcut in the British Museum, reproduced British Library (Bibl. F4), no. 127, which shows at deck level a banner of Howard's arms. See also the illustrations reproduced in H. Y. Thompson, ed., *Lord Howard of Effingham and the Spanish Armada*, Roxburghe Club 1919.

19 *Relation of the Voyage to Cadiz 1596*, by Sir William Slyngesbie, in *Naval Miscellany* I, NRS 20, 1902, pp. 25-92. The flags are illustrated by Perrin (Bibl. C23) plate IX, 3, 4 & 5, as Elizabethan ensigns. It is not clear from the manuscript whether any means was adopted of distinguishing the private ships of the fleet by squadrons. It would be interesting to know which was the earliest European navy to indicate three grades of flag officer by flags flown at the different mastheads.

20 Perrin (Bibl. C23), p. 58; Pepys MS. 2877, p. 417. Sergeant Knight rightly thought that the quarterly version of the Union Flag was used early in James I's reign. A chart attributed to Thomas Hood and dated 1604 has a cartouche with two quarterly Unions: R. A. Skelton, *Maps and Architectural Drawings . . . at Hatfield House*, Roxburghe Club 1971, no. 2. There seem also to have been variants of the royal arms at the beginning of James I's reign: an engraved portrait of the king by Laurence Johnson, dated 1603, includes a shield of arms arranged: 1, England; 2, Scotland; 3, France; 4, Ireland (A.M. Hind, *Engraving in England in the Sixteenth and Seventeenth Centuries*, Cambridge 1952-64, II, p.35, pl.10).

21 An undated manuscript in the National Library of Scotland, MS. 2517, fol. 67-8, contains drawings of seven alternative designs for combining the crosses of St George and St Andrew, not including the design eventually chosen. It is annotated by the Earl of Nottingham (formerly Howard of Effingham) who noted a preference for a design impaling the crosses; 'for this is like man and wife without blemish on [one] another'. On the 'Scotch Union' see W. Smith, 'The Scots Union Flag', *FB* 12 (1973), pp. 55–8; Perrin (Bibl. C23), pp. 56-7.

22 For the quarterly version (despite Fig. 11) see Pepys MS. 2877, p. 417; Perrin (Bibl. C23), pp. 56-7. The impaled version is recorded in the Journal of M. H. Tromp, 31 October 1643, Algemeen Rijksarchief, The Hague, Archieven der Admiraliteitscolleges XLVII, no. 1, fol. 291. I owe this reference to Dr R. E. J. Weber. See *MM* 9 (1923), p. 254.

23 An early dated illustration of the use of the Union Flag at sea is the bizarre fantasy painting of the restoration of St Paul's Cathedral, now in the Society of Antiquaries of London, which was devised by Henry Farley and painted by John Gipkyn in 1616. It shows a ship with the Union at the main.

24 Perrin (Bibl. C23), p. 59.

25 T. W. Fulton, *The Sovereignty of the Sea*, Edinburgh & London 1911; S. R. Gardiner & C. T. Atkinson, *Letters and Papers Relating to the First Dutch War*, I, NRS 13, 1899, pp. 170-298; *Sir William Monson's Tracts*, 4, NRS 45, 1913, pp. 119-27. Compare Boteler's comments (Appendix B, p. 95).

26 Perrin (Bibl. C23), pp. 89-90, 92, 96, 98.

27 The ensigns of the period illustrated in Plate I are from other contemporary sources; no. 15 from the plan of Baffin's voyage to North America in 1615, BL Add. MS. 12206, fol. 6a; no. 16 from William Simpson's 1626 chart of Portland, NMM G223: 2/91.

28 Perrin (Bibl. C23), pp. 115-17. Simpson's chart (see note 27) shows, as well as striped ensigns, a red one and a red one with a diagonal white flash reaching from the canton to the lower fly corner, each with St George in the canton.

29 Perrin (Bibl. C23), pp. 89-91, 115.

30 See p. 58, and note 116.

31 Wilson (Bibl. B36); Knighton (Bibl. F10). Some important naval manuscripts once owned by Pepys are among the Rawlinson MSS. in the Bodleian Library, Oxford: see C. H. Firth, 'Papers relating to the Navy in the Bodleian Library', *MM* 3 (1913), pp. 225-9.

32 Perrin (Bibl. C23), pp. 62-3. A copy of the order of February 1649, bearing Cromwell's signature, is NMM MS. ADL/A/16.

33 The cross and harp command flag was already in use in 1650; see G. Penn, *Memorials of Sir William Penn*, London 1833, I, p. 314.

34 King (Bibl. B18), p. 145. A similar command flag is shown in the drawing of the battle of Scheveningen by the Elder Van de Velde in the Rijksmuseum, Amsterdam, no. 2225.

35 Pepys had the testimony of Mr Homewood that 'the Generals at Sea before the Restauration wore a Standard of the Harp and Cross in a laurel at his maintop masthead, the Vice Admiral the plain harp and cross at his Foretop and the Rear Admiral at the mizzen top' (Pepys MS. 2877, p. 379). The flag came to the National Maritime Museum on the dispersal of the Museum of the RUSI in 1963. Technical examination by Mrs Karen Finch, in whose workshops the flag was cleaned in 1980, suggested that it has never been flown at sea. A similar flag is shown in Zeeman's oil painting of a First Dutch War action, now in the Scheepvaart Museum, Amsterdam. See King (Bibl. B18), pp. 144-5. The escutcheons on the flag are what one would normally think of as upside-down.

36 Perrin (Bibl. C23), pp. 92-4, 117-18. The system of squadron distinction may not have operated in practice: the two large

drawings in the Rijksmuseum by the Elder Van de Velde of the battle of Scheveningen show the English ships without pennants. For discussion of the reasons for the change in the seniority of colours see Naval Historical Library, Search 185/11.

37 Perrin (Bibl. C23), p. 65. I have not found any authority for Perrin's statement that the Cross and Harp jack was restored in 1659.

38 Pepys (Bibl. F16),. I, pp. 136-7. Pepys's wording suggests that the fleet had jacks and flags consisting of the Union with a harp over the centre. See Barlow's description of the *Naseby* a few days later (quoted p. 22). See also note 46.

39 Normal English practice differed from Dutch in that all the English ships flew pennants at the main, whereas the Dutch flew them at different mastheads, according to squadron; and the English flagships normally struck their pennants on hoisting an admiral's flag, which the Dutch did not.

40 Perrin (Bibl. C23), pp. 81-5; H. S. London, 'Official Badges', *Coat of Arms* 4 (1956-7), pp. 94-5; R. M. Blomfield, 'The Admiralty Flag, *Journal of the RUSI* 38 (1894), pp. 1305-14, and 'Origin and History of the Admiralty Badges', *ibid.*, pp. 133-41. There have been numerous variations over the years in the run of the cable on the anchor flag; see A. P. Herbert, 'The foul anchor', *Coat of Arms* 6 (1960-1), pp. 101-3; and *Errata* 4 (1920) to the Admiralty Flag book (Bibl. B9), 1915. Over the last hundred years the field has usually been represented as crimson rather than scarlet.

41 Edward Barlow, *Journal*, ed. B. Lubbock, London 1934, I, p. 43. Although Barlow's *Journal* was written some years after 1660, the specific description here seems likely to be accurate. James was nominated Lord High Admiral on 16 May 1660. The quotation from Barlow is Lubbock's modernized text, corrected by reference to the rather garbled original.

42 NMM (Bibl. F13), no. 109; see Peacock (Bibl. C22), p. 272; Perrin (Bibl. C23), p. 81. Compare NMM (Bibl. F13), no. 134 The present authority for the use of the three flags on the Royal Yacht *Britannia* is an Admiralty Circular of 4 July 1833.

43 Logs of HMS *Centurion* 1748-52, NMM MS. ADM/L/C 85, 31 October 1750. On launching flags see C. H. Gaye-Hexham, 'Launching flags in HM ships', *MM* 36 (1950), pp. 229-32. A drawing by Van de Velde the Elder of the launching of the *Woolwich* in 1675 shows the Royal Standard amidships and the anchor flag on the forecastle (reprod. F. Fox, *Great Ships*, Greenwich 1980, p. 143).

44 Pepys MS. 2877, p. 384; Peacock (Bibl. C22), pp. 273-4. A letter to Pepys from the Navy Office dated 6 September 1686, PRO, ADM 1/3555, p. 881, makes it clear that this special crowned anchor flag was for use at the fore when the Royal Standard was at the main. Compare NMM (Bibl. F14), I, no. 610, p. 393. Before 1673 James used the anchor flag on his

yacht; see Barlow's *Journal* (cited note 41), I, pp. 147-8 (1668). For the use of the flag of the Admiral of Scotland, see Boymans-van Beuningen Museum (Bibl. F3), p. 63, pl. 246, 247. The blue and white anchor flag is given as the 'Scots Admls Flag' in the Graydon flag book (Bibl. A5), p. 3. James was appointed Admiral of Scotland on 1 February 1673.

45 For the special flags used by William and Mary in 1677, see below, note 154.

46 NMM (Bibl. F14), I, p. 42, 165; G. La Roërie, 'A propos des pavillons des yachts anglais', *Bulletin de l'Association des Amis du Musée de la Marine*, no. 13 (1934), pp. 175-7; C. King, 'Les pavillons du yacht royal anglais au Musée de la Marine', *ibid.*, no. 21 (1936), pp. 2-7; *MM* 37 (1951), pp. 318-9; *MM* 43 (1957), pp. 279-80. It is possible that Charles II himself disliked the use of the harp as the emblem of Ireland: see Pepys's *Diary*, 13 May 1660, cited above, p. 21; Sergeant Knight thought the harp 'no more the Armse of that Kingdome . . . than any other Constellation or any of the Signes in the Zodiack' (Pepys MS. 2877, p. 423).

47 For example Corbett (Bibl. C8), p. 165; compare Perrin (Bibl. C23), p. 98.

48 For the order about the pennant for the Downs, see PRO, ADM 2/1, fol. 182, letter of 12 December 1674 from Derby House. Up to about this date junior captains apparently took in their pennants in the presence of a senior captain so that the senior captain's masthead pennant became a virtual pennant of command. See NMM (Bibl. F14), I, p. 28. For the 'Budgee' pennant of 1690 see *MM* 1 (1911), p. 59. The use of broad pennants in the 18th century requires further research. The original purpose of the appointment of commodores was to relieve pressure on the nine active flag officers of the fleet. See also R. M. Blomfield, 'Commadore or Commodore?', *MM* 4 (1914), pp. 73-7.

49 This is a simplification of the rather complex variations on the white ensign in Queen Anne's reign, for which see Perrin (Bibl. C23), pp. 100-1, 118. Compare the white ensigns portrayed in Plate IX.

50 At the end of the 17th century pennants were still quite broad, up to three foot (nearly a metre), at the hoist; they later became narrower, and the modern 'whip pennant' is only four inches (10cm) across the hoist. The tricolour pennants were split at the fly; the plain pennants usually not. By the 19th century tricolour pennants, too, were being made in the modern shape with a pointed end. See the examples illustrated in Snider (Bibl. C27), dating from the Anglo-American War of 1812, which are not split at the fly. However, an authoritative-looking flag book of *c*. 1830 (Bibl. A31) illustrates a tricolour pennant split at the fly, and stipulates that it be 18 foot long. The distinction pennants of the late 17th century were as a rule 'two cloths broader at the staff' than ordinary pennants: PRO, ADM 1/3555, p. 847, letter of 2 August 1686 from the Navy Office to Pepys; I owe this reference to Michael Robinson.

51 Special distinguishing vanes can be seen in Nicholas Pocock's oil painting of the Battle of the Saints, 1782, in the NMM; see H. P. Mead, 'Some remarks on squadronal colours and ships' distinguishing vanes', *MM* 23 (1937), pp. 502-3.

52 Corbett (Bibl. C8), p. 251; and Bibl. C9, p. 300. Drake and Hood were both Rear Admirals of the Blue at the battle: Hood, the second in command, hoisted a red command flag instead of his blue one.

53 *MM* 4 (1914), p. 272.

54 King (Bibl. C15), p. 103; see *Queen's Regulations* (Bibl. C26), para. 1216; compare, however, *Admiralty Manual* (Bibl. C1), p. 361. For the hoisting of the Union Jack in harbour, see *MM* 60 (1974), pp. 437-8.

55 Hayes-McCoy (Bibl. C11) pp. 36-41. Early illustrations of the Irish saltire flag are in Van der Dussen (Bibl. A4) and Allard (Bibl. A9). For its use as the flag of Jersey, see *MM* 37 (1951), pp. 82-4; *Heraldry Gazette*, November 1981; *Flagmaster* 35 (1981); 36 (1982).

56 A. W. B. Messenger 'The Union Flag, *Coat of Arms* 2 (1952-3), pp. 95-100; J. A. Stewart, 'The Design of the Union Flag', *Coat of Arms* 2 (1952-3), pp. 125-7; J. Joy, 'On the Union Flag', *FB* 12 (1973-4), pp. 44-54; L. Loynes, 'British Flag Proportions', *FB* 12 (1973-4), pp. 84-5; Purves (Bibl. C25); Barraclough & Wilson (Bibl. C4).

57 For a detailed account of the development of the British royal arms see Pinches and Pinches (Bibl. F17).

58 N. H. Nicolas, *Dispatches and Letters of Lord Viscount Nelson*, London 1844-6, VII, p. 104.

59 Perrin (Bibl. C23), pp. 106-7.

60 For the reasons for the abandonment of the squadronal system and the adoption by the Royal Navy of the white colours, see the account in Naval Historical Library, Search 185/11; also Admiral Sir F. W. Grey, 'The distinctive flags of the British Navy', a manuscript dated 1864 in the Naval Historical Library (Pamphlets Vol. 480). The first edition of the *Queen's Regulations* to omit mention of the tricolour pennant is the edition of 1861; however it is not included in Le Gras, *Album des Pavillons* (1858) (Bibl. A34), or in the careful flag book dated 1845 in the Naval Historical Library (Bibl. A33).

61 Perrin (Bibl. C23), pp. 100-2.

62 C. King, 'Flags in the War', *Yachting Monthly* 27 (1919), pp. 304-15, Mead (Bibl. C18), pp. 89-92; *MM* 23 (1937), pp. 229-30. The relevant orders are gathered together in the Naval Historical Library, Search 185/12.

63 Hakluyt (Bibl. F8), VII, p. 143; Perrin (Bibl. C23), pp. 45-6; J. Sottas, 'An Atlas of Drake's Last Voyage', *MM* 2 (1912),

pp. 135-42. For the visual evidence on the flags flown on Drake's voyage to the West Indies in 1585-6, see British Library (Bibl. F4), nos. 114-22. I know of no specific evidence for the flags flown on the *Golden Hind* on Drake's voyage round the World. For the 'Drake' flags at Buckland Abbey, see p. 92 and note 150.

64 Pepys MS. 2877, pp. 279, 315, 377.

65 King (Bibl. B18), p. 146; and *MM* 9 (1923), p. 256.

66 Mead, Bibl. C17; and C18, pp. 8-28; Naval Historical Library, Search 185/41: 'Memorandum about the Merchant Service Ensign and Jack 1674-1879' (copy in NMM Library).

67 *Queen's Regulations* (Bibl. C26), para. 1252.

68 Mead (Bibl. C18), pp. 63-6.

69 E. Corlett, *The Iron Ship*, Bradford on Avon 1975, pp. 113-4.

70 Hakluyt (Bibl. F8), V, pp. 196-7.

71 Rijksmuseum (Bibl. B28), no. 112. Compare the flags with red and yellow chequered borders on the group of ships illustrated in BL, Add. MS. 5023, fol. 1, a drawing which probably dates from the 1680s.

72 A range of East India Company flags is shown in two other oil paintings in the NMM, one of the East India Yard at Deptford, attributed to Sailmaker (reproduced in F. Fox, *Great Ships*, Greenwich 1980. col. pl. II); the other a ship portrait by Peter Monamy, which shows the Company pennant. On the flags of the East India Co. and the 'Bombay Marine' see Perrin (Bibl. C23) pp. 124, 130-1; E. Cotton (ed. by C. Fawcett), *East Indiamen*, London 1949, Chap. 4; C. Fawcett, 'The striped flag of the East India Company and its connexion with the American 'Stars and Stripes', *MM* 23 (1937), pp. 449-76; A. Rowand, *The Naval and Maritime Flags of British India* (typescript 1909, NMM Library). Another version of the ensign had a cross of St George through the fly; this is said to have been the distinctive ensign of armed vessels and privateers of the Company, but exactly how and over what period it was used is not entirely clear.

73 A. C. Wardle (Bibl. E10), pp. 161-3. For Bidston Hill on Liverpool creamware pottery, see K. Boney 'Bidston Hill in Pottery Decoration', *Apollo* 75 (1961), pp. 37-40; B. Rackham, *Catalogue of the Schreiber Collection* (Victoria & Albert Museum 1924-30), II, pp. 82-3. An oil painting by R. Salmon belonging to Merseyside County Museums, dated 1822, shows the masts on Bidston Hill.

74 B. Lubbock, *The Blackwall Frigates*, Glasgow 1922, p. 47.

75 Loughran (Bibl. E4), pp. 93-7.

76 There is a history of the flags of the Board of Ordnance by J. W. Steeple in *MM* 46 (1960), pp. 23-8; see also G. A. Viner *Ordnance Flags*, 1960.

77 Bibl. B9.

78 The material in this paragraph is taken from A. A. Purves, 'Flags for Revenue Cutters and Cruisers', *Model Shipwright*, 27 (1979), pp. 48-51, where the flags are illustrated. See also *MM* 17 (1931), p. 283.

79 A. W. Robertson, *A History of the Ship Letters of the British Isles*, privately printed 1955, pp. A55-6; B frontispiece; B3-4. Some drawings of Falmouth packet flags *c.* 1802 are in the NMM (ref. SGN/E/4); and copies of other drawings of Falmouth packet flags of *c.* 1796-7 and *c.* 1819 are among the papers of Basil Lubbock, also in the NMM (ref. LUB/40).

80 H. G. Carr, 'Flags of the Corporation of Trinity House', *MM* 43 (1957), pp. 39-45; Mead (Bibl. C18), pp. 96-7; 'Trinity House and the White Ensign'. *Shipbuilding and Shipping Record*, 8 October 1959, p. 277; *Model Shipwright* 10 (1974), pp. 141-4. For the flags of the main British public authorities see Barraclough & Crampton (Bibl. B5), pp. 42-8.

81 Perrin (Bibl. C23), pp. 124-6.

82 D. Phillips-Birt, *The Cumberland Fleet*, London 1978, p. 96. A number of historic yacht flags are preserved at the Royal Thames Yacht Club.

83 Perrin (Bibl. C23), pp. 136-9; Naval Historical Library, Search 185/48; *Parliamentary Papers*, 1859 (session 2), Vol. 26, pp. 405-24. The Elder Brethren of Trinity House were in 1894 granted Admiralty permission 'to fly the White Ensign of H. M. Fleet on board their steam and sailing vessels upon all occasions upon which the ships are dressed, and while escorting Her Majesty in company with Royal yachts and ships of war'; see references cited above, note 80.

84 For the use of flags by yachts, see Barraclough (Bibl. C3); Irving (Bibl. C13); Stewart (Bibl. C28); B. Heckstall Smith, 'A treatise on the etiquette of flags', *Yachting World*, supplement, 29 April 1932; R. L. Hewitt, *Yacht Flags and Signals*, Royal Yachting Association, 4th ed., 1979; G. H. Burrows, 'Burgees', *Coat of Arms* 9 (1966-7), pp. 21-9. The privilege ensigns of yacht clubs, their burgees, and the personal flags of yacht owners were listed until 1960 in *Lloyds Register of Yachts* and for some years after that in a separate supplement; this is no longer published.

85 *MM* 27 (1941), p. 264. On pirate flags generally, see H. G. Carr, 'Pirate Flags', *MM* 29 (1943), pp. 131-4.

86 G. F. Dow and J. H. Edmonds, *Pirates of the New England Coast*, Salem 1923, p. 308.

87 Captain Charles Johnson (probably an alias of Daniel Defoe), *A General History of the Robberies and Murders of the Most Notorious Pyrates*, 3rd ed., London 1725, facing p. 259. The text and plate of the first edition (1724) are different in the detail of the flags.

88 In J. Oosterwyk's 1716 edition of Allard's book (Bibl. A9); also in the 1737 *Connoissance des Pavillons* (Bibl. A20).

89 A. P. McGowan, *Sailor*, London 1977, pp. 122-3. A number of 'Jolly Roger' submarine flags are at the Royal Naval Submarine Museum, HMS *Dolphin*, Gosport.

90 See Chapin (Bibl. D54); Furlong & McCandless (Bibl. D57), pp. 38-40.

91 See Chapin (Bibl. D53). The globe shown in some early flag books is apparently an error due to careless copying of a badly drawn tree; however, some 18th-century flag books, such as the 1705 edition of Allard (Bibl. A9, Part 2, p. 21), include the explanation that the globe is the symbol of the New World. In the signal book of *c.* 1756, Bibl. A22, the emblem is interpreted as a human face.

92 G. W. Allen, *A Naval History of the American Revolution*, Boston & New York 1913, pp. 64-5.

93 Perrin (Bibl. C23), pp. 127-8.

94 This is a much discussed question. See, as well as most books on American flags, C. Fawcett, 'The striped flag of the East India Company and its connexion with the Stars and Stripes', *MM* 23 (1937), pp. 449-76.

95 J. P. Jones, *Memoir*, ed. G. W. Gawalt, Washington, DC, 1979, p. 5. On the signals used by Hopkins's fleet, see Preble (Bibl. D60), pp. 232-3. Compare Furlong & McCandless (Bibl. D57), p. 90.

96 See F. McMaster, 'The Ensign of the Continental Brigantine *Lexington* 1777', *Military Collector and Historian, Journal of the Company of Military Historians*, 26 (1974), pp. 224-5; Furlong & McCandless (Bibl. D57), pp. 92-3.

97 Quaife (Bibl. D61), pp. 39-40; Furlong & McCandless (Bibl. D57), pp. 98-101.

98 Quaife (Bibl. D61), p. 41.

99 Quaife (Bibl. D61), pp. 38, 41-7; S. E. Morison, *John Paul Jones*, Boston 1959, pp. 423-5. The painting of the action itself made in 1781 by Nicholas Pocock (*MM* 67 (1981), pp. 194-5) shows the *Bonhomme Richard* and the *Alliance* with a Stars and Stripes striped red and white.

100 Preble (Bibl. D60), pp. 347, 349. A circular of May 1818 arranging the stars in four staggered rows was altered at the instance of the President in a further circular of September 1818, which laid down the pattern in Fig. 70.

101 See Smith (Bibl. D65), pp. 79, 81, for the current official specification. Up to about 1916 smaller vessels and boats of the U.S. navy were in the habit of using a form of the ensign which the number of stars was reduced to 13; see Cooper (Bibl. D55), p. vii.

102 The thirteen star design was laid down in 1866; see Preble (Bibl. D60), p. 674. From 13 October 1975 to 31 December 1976 the U.S. navy used as a jack, in honour of the bicentennial of the American Revolution, a flag of seven red and six white stripes with a rattlesnake and the motto DON'T TREAD ON ME across it - the supposed 'First Navy Jack'; see *FB* 15 (1976), pp. 180-1.

103 This paragraph is much condensed from the account in Lyman (Bibl. D58); see also Preble (Bibl. D60), pp. 659-74. An official guide to flag usage in the U.S. navy is *Flags, pennants and colors* (Bibl. D56).

104 Rijksmuseum (Bibl. B27), nos. 107-9. Although 17th and 18th-century flag books tend to show the arms of the ragged cross extending to the corners of the flag, the arms of the cross on actual flags seem frequently to have been rounded off just short of the corners.

105 P. Lux-Wurm, 'Columbus: what was his flag?', *FB* 8 (1969) pp. 75-6.

106 Siegel (Bibl. B29), pp. 100-2; Fernandez Duro (Bibl. D41), pp. 467-661; *MM* 10 (1924), pp. 329-32; *FB* 7 (1968), pp. 101-4; Perrin (Bibl. C23), p. 112; F. Sarre and O. Neubecker, 'Die Seeschlacht von Lepanto', *Jahrbuch der preussischen Kunstsammlungen*, 59 (1938), pp. 233-46.

107 C. Fernandez Duro, *La Armada Invencible*, Madrid 1884-5, II, pp. 82, 220; and Bibl. D41, pp. 296-8; F. Pigafetta, *Discorso . . . sopra l'ordinanza dell'Armata Catholica*, Rome 1588, 'Nelle bandiere & ne' Gonfaloni, & Flamuli, & pennoni de' Navili non e effigiato altro che il Crocifisso, co'l motto DOMINE DISCERNE CAUSAM TUAM . . . l'imagine della Vergine Madre di Dio, co'l motto DEMONSTRA TE ESSE MATREM'.

108 See Vicente Cascante (Bibl. D50), pp. 487-560; *FB* 21 (1982), p. 49, for an account of more recent changes in the national arms of Spain as represented on flags. Charles III (who reigned 1759-88) included with the collar of the Order of the Golden Fleece the collar of his Order of Charles III. On the vexed question of whether the Leon lion is red or purple see Vicente Cascante, pp. 561-605.

109 Translated from Almirall Fusté (Bibl. D39), p. 49.

110 Translated from Almirall Fusté (Bibl. D39), p. 53.

111 The coat of arms was modified in 1981; see *Flagmaster* 36 (March 1982); *FB* 21 (1982), pp. 43-56.

112 On the complicated early history of the tricolour and the reasons for the change from orange to red in the upper stripe see Waard (Bibl. D34); Jonker (Bibl. D26); Cannenburg (Bibl. D23); Sierksma (Bibl. D31), p. 135. At various times in Dutch history the colours have been a matter of debate: in the 1930s a right-wing-inspired movement to make the colours orange/white/light blue developed. A royal decree in 1937 confirmed the colours as red/white/dark blue, and the colours were technically defined in 1949.

113 N. Witsen, *Aeloude en hedendaegsche Scheepsbouw*, Amsterdam 1671, p. 272. On the same page Witsen gives details of flag sizes for the different rates of Dutch warship.

114 Normally the initial of the company chamber was added to the VOC and GWC monograms, e.g. A for Amsterdam, or D for Delft. On flags supposed to have represented the different chambers of the East India Company, see Pama (Bibl. D29), pp. 13-15.

115 For example a painting by Storck in the Nederlands Scheepvaart Museum, Amsterdam, and an etching by Zeeman of the *Swarte Beer* (Bartsch, V, p. 139, no. 7).

116 NMM (Bibl. F14); Boymans-van Beuningen Museum (Bibl. F3); also British Museum (Bibl. F5), I, pp. 486-534. Compare the drawings attributed to T. Phillips of the Third Dutch War battles of Solebay and Texel, owned by the Earl of Dartmouth and deposited on loan at the NMM (Fig. 17; see the facsimile edited by J. Corbett, NRS 1908). The flag arrangements of the fleets of the First Dutch War are more obscure. Dr R. E. J. Weber has kindly referred me to Maarten Tromp's fighting instructions of May 1653 in the Algemeen Rijksarchief, The Hague, Coll. van Wassenaar, Acq. 1891, no. 28, VI, bbb: according to these, Tromp's squadron had pennants at the main, Jan Evertsen's pennants at the fore, Witte de With's jacks at the spritsail topmast, de Ruyter's pennants at the mizzen peak, P. Floriszoon's pennants at the mizzen. Compare NMM (Bibl. F14), I, pp. 119-20, and the two large drawings by the Elder Van de Velde of the battle of Scheveningen (Ter Heide) in the Rijksmuseum, Amsterdam, no. 2074 and no. 2225; also the grisaille in the NMM (NMM, Bibl. F13, no. 11), of which Fig. 14 is a detail.

117 Cannenburg (Bibl. D23), pp. 407-8; Pama (Bibl. D29), ch. 3. The motive for the change was probably to differentiate the flag from the flag of Holland. Early in the War of Independence from Spain the lion held seventeen arrows for the seventeen provinces. The number of arrows varied with the number of provinces in the Union.

118 Translated from Treu (Bibl. D32). See also Smith (Bibl. B34), p. 162.

119 For a short period after 1795 the navy of the Batavian Republic used a system on the British model of dividing flag officers into red, white and blue. The NMM also has an ensign taken at Camperdown and the painted panel of a third flag (Fig. 81), said to have been taken during the Walcheren campaign in 1809; however, it is doubtful whether the design was still in use as late as 1809.

120 G. Fournier, *Hydrographie*, Paris 1643, pp. 795-6.

121 Quoted from King (Bibl. D13), p. 6. The text is slightly ambiguous, but it is no doubt the plain blue flag with a white cross (without the royal arms) that is described as 'l'ancient Pavillon de la Nation Françoise', to which the royal arms are now to be added.

122 Translated from *Ordonnance de Louis XIV pour les Armées navales et Arcenaux de Marine*, Paris 1689.

123 Bibl. A7, p. 565; Compare N. Aubin, *Dictionnaire de Marine*, Amsterdam 1716, p. 689: 'On voit souvent au mât d'artimon des vaisseaux marchands de petits pavillons où sont les armes du lieu, de la ville où le maitre fait son domicile; & au mât d'avant les armes du lieu ou demeurent les Afreteurs'.

124 Pasch (Bibl. D15). The official ban on the use of plain white colours by merchant ships remained in force, albeit ineffectively, until 1765, when the long-standing practice was sanctioned.

125 According to *L'Art de Batir les Vaisseaux* (Bibl. A19), p. 15, the *Pavillon Royal* could be used by 'Le Vaisseau Amiral de France'; but see King (Bibl. D11), pp. 291-2; J. de la Varende, *Le Maréchal de Tourville et son temps*, Paris 1943, p. 127.

126 King (Bibl. D13), p. 10; see the oil painting in NMM by Nicholas Pocock of the Battle of Frigate Bay. A detailed account of the French squadronal distinctions in the Battle of Ushant in 1778 is in National Maritime Museum MS.REC/46. There was a 'blue squadron' in the French fleet at La Hogue in 1692; see *Naval Records* (Catalogue of an Exhibition at the Public Record Office), 1950, no. 29. See further Naval Historical Library, Search 185/11.

127 King (Bibl. D12); also, the same author, 'Fresh evidence concerning the French jacks of 1790', *MM* 18 (1932), pp. 229-40.

128 M. Loir, *Études d'histoire maritime*, Paris & Nancy 1901, pp. 56-7. See Fig. 85. For a useful brief account of the later history of the Tricolour, see Smith (Bibl. B34), pp. 135-8.

129 Perrin (Bibl. C23), p. 155.

130 Hakluyt (Bibl. F8), VII, p. 324.

131 Perrin (Bibl. C23), pp. 193-4.

132 NMM ref. SIG/A/1.

133 Probably the earliest English signal book to survive is Bodleian Library, Oxford, MS. Rawl. C 512, dated 1695. It contains drawings of ships making various signals, with their meanings indicated. It is marked 'George Graydon' on the cover; George Graydon (perhaps a relative of John Graydon, compiler of the flag book in the Pepys Library) was commissioned Lieutenant on 5 August 1696 (R. D. Merriman, *The Sergison Papers*, NRS 89, 1950, p. 359).

134 NMM ref. SIG/B/1.

135 H. P. Mead, 'The Earliest English Signal Book', *United States Naval Institute Proceedings*, 61 (no. 361, 1935), pp. 1819-25. A 'dictionary' of flag signals, with coloured drawings of flags, guns and lights, is included in a sumptuous manuscript volume of *Instructions* in the Naval Historical Library, ref. Ec 48, which dates from *c.* 1689; see Perrin (Bibl. C23), p. 162.

136 NMM, MS.SIG/B/6 is an example. Instructions on making your own signal book are in R. Liddell, *The Seaman's new Vade Mecum*, London 1787, p. 261.

137 NMM MSS. HOL/21 and HOL/22; SIG/A/8.

138 NMM ref. MKH/31.

139 The literature on the history of British naval signalling is particularly copious for the period *c.* 1775-1815. See Corbett (Bibl. C8 and C9); Perrin (Bibl. C23), pp. 166-75; Mead (Bibl. C19); Holland (Bibl. C12); Tunstall (Bibl. F20); Woods (Bibl. B38). See also 'Maritime signals', *United Services Journal* 1836, part I, pp. 289-97. The successive sets of numerary flags in the naval codes from 1790 to 1810 are conveniently tabulated by Perrin (Bibl. C23), pl. XIII.

140 See N. H. Nicolas, *Dispatches and Letters of Lord Viscount Nelson* (London 1844-6), VII, p. 150. See also *FB* 21 (1982), p. 171-6. On John Roome, the signalman who is supposed to have hoisted the signal, see 'A Hero of Trafalgar', *The PD Review*, No. 93 (Jan. 1953), pp. 19-20.

141 On the 19th-century Royal Navy signal books see 'The General Signal Book of 1859', *Naval Science* 2 (1873), pp. 176-81. For more recent developments see Mead & 'Buccaneer' (Bibl. C20). See also *FB* 21 (1982), pp. 177-88.

142 H. P. Mead, 'Captain Frederick Marryat, R.N.', *United States Naval Institute Proceedings*, vol. 59 (no. 361, 1933), pp. 371-5; C. Lloyd, *Captain Marryat and the Old Navy* (London 1939), pp. 176-81. The library at the NMM contains a variety of other specialized and private signal codes, including some private yacht club codes of the first half of the 19th century.

143 This explanation appears in the early editions of the *Commercial Code*. See H. P. Mead 'The History of the International Code', *United States Naval Institute Proceedings*, vol. 60 (no. 378, 1934), pp. 1083-8.

144 *MM* 65 (1979), p. 87. See also Naval Historical Library, Search 185/36.

145 6 George IV, cap. 78, section VIII. Compare Mead (Bibl. C18), pp. 81-2. The yellow flag was already in use as a Quarantine flag in 1806; see the log of HMS *Superb* for 13 May 1806, NMM, MS. ADM/L/5/540.

146 H. R. Wagner, *Sir Francis Drake's Voyage round the World*, San Francisco 1926, p. 374.

147 See H. P. Mead, 'The Art of Dressing Ship', *The Navy*, 2 (Feb. 1955), pp. 38-9, 51; and Bibl. C18, pp. 53-63. For two other illustrations of ships dressed overall see *Country Life Annual*, 1969, p. 59 (Queen Adelaide's visit to Malta, 1839);

and B. Stewart, *The Library and Picture Collection of the Port of London Authority,* London 1955, p. 35 (The Opening of St Katherine Dock, 1828). Rules for the occasions on which Royal Navy ships dress ship are printed in the current *Queen's Regulations* (Bibl. C26), para. 1240, and the order of flags was printed in the *Visual Signalling Handbook* (Bibl. C29; this is no longer current). Notes on dressing ship in privately owned vessels are found in Barraclough (Bibl. C3), pp. 45-9 and endpapers. See also J. Vichot, 'Le pavois', *Neptunia* 101 (1971), pp. 5-16.

148 It is difficult to know what kind of fabric was meant at a particular date by words such as 'tuke', 'buckram', 'say', and 'bewpers' which are used to describe flags in the 16th and 17th centuries, but it is clear that flags were made of various and sometimes expensive materials: see Perrin (Bibl. C23), pp. 42-6: Oppenheim (Bibl. F15), p. 41.

149 J. K. Laughton, *Defeat of the Spanish Armada*, II, NRS 2, 1894, pp. 242-9, 320-1.

150 Perrin (Bibl. C23), pp. 45-6. Important survivals of the type of banner mentioned in Elizabethan inventories are the painted silk flags associated with Sir Francis Drake preserved at Buckland Abbey in Devon. These flags deserve to be more fully studied. There are opinions on their date and the putative link with Drake in Victoria and Albert Museum Registered Papers 1953/3117 and National Maritime Museum, Callender papers. See also S.E. Borrett, 'The Drake colours', *Military Modelling*, April 1984, p. 288, where six of the eight flags are interpreted as regimental colours; I owe this reference to James Barber.

151 Rijksmuseum (Bibl. B28), nos. 110-25.

152 A certain Mrs Venner is stated to have been the exclusive contractor to the navy from 1626 to 1649 by E. Berckman, *The Hidden Navy*, London 1973, pp. 62-3. Pepys's *Diary* includes a number of references to John Young and Henry Whistler, contractors for the supply of flags to the Royal Navy; see the index to Pepys (Bibl. F16).

153 Pepys's *Diary*, 5 October 1664; 7 October 1664; 27 November 1664; 28 January 1665; 24 September 1666.

154 Pepys, *Admiralty Journal*, NRS 57, 1923, pp. 550, 566, and Pepys MS. 2877, p. 270. The flags were designed by Sir William Dugdale, Garter King of Arms; compare British Museum (Bibl. F5), Van de Velde, no. 42.

155 BL, Harl. MS. 253, fol. 66.

156 Perrin (Bibl. C23), p. 45. Seven of the eight 'Drake' flags at Buckland Abbey are approximately seven feet (2.1 metres) square; the eighth is approximately 7 feet 6 inches broad and 3 feet 6 inches long (2.3 by 1.1 metres).

157 Quoted from Perrin (Bibl. C23), p. 201.

158 PRO, ADM 106/3542, box 1, pkt 24; cf. Bodleian Library, MS. Rawl. C 914, p. 52.

159 Pepys MS. 2877, pp. 367, 382.

160 Rijksmuseum (Bibl. B28), no. 118.

161 NMM MS. CHA/F/39, letter of 29 November 1822.

162 NMM MS. ADM/BP/10, letter of 2 July 1790. A note adds: 'By a Breadth is meant the distanse from seam to seam in the usual way of making flags and not the Brd of a Cloth of Bunting, which is what is called two Brds.'

163 On the methods of attaching flags see Perrin (Bibl. C23), pp. 199-200; King (Bibl. C15), pp. 101-3; Callender (Bibl. F6), pp. 49-52.

164 See *Catalogue of House Flags . . . displayed in the Poplar Recreation Ground on the Occasion of the Coronation of King George V,* London 1911.

165 There is conflicting evidence on the colours of the ensigns of the ships of Howe's fleet in this battle. See Perrin (Bibl. C23), p. 120; O. Warner, *The Glorious First of June*, London 1961, pp. 81, 110.

166 *Fairburn's Edition of the Funeral of Admiral Lord Nelson,* London 1806, p. 95.

Glossary

This brief glossary is not a complete guide to flag terminology, which remains chaotic despite attempts in recent years to standardize it (for instance, Smith, Bibl. B34, pp. 12-31; Bibl. B13). The terminology and spellings adopted in this book are a series of compromises between the technical languages of the Royal Navy and of heraldry, the English of the 'landlubber', and the usages of international 'vexillology'.

Argent
The heraldic term for white or silver.

Azure
The heraldic term for blue.

Badge
'Badges are heraldic insignia which, like arms and crests, are distinctive of a person or a family, but unlike them are not associated with the shield or helm' (Boutell, Bibl. F2, p. 163). See A. C. Fox-Davies, *Heraldic Badges*, London 1907; H. S. London 'Official Badges', *Coat of Arms* 4 (1956-7) pp. 93-100.

Banner
A term often loosely used of flags of rectangular shape and lavish design. Strictly speaking a 'banner' is a rectangular flag with arms and no other charge upon it; See Boutell (Bibl. F2), pp. 252-4. Compare *Standard*.

Barge flags
On the barge flags of London livery companies, see H. G. Carr, 'Barge flags of the City Livery Companies of London', *MM* 28 (1942), pp. 222-30.

Battle ensign
Ensigns used by warships in action, when it is customary to hoist additional ensigns in case one is shot away.

Bewpers
The woollen cloth of which British sea flags were made in the 17th century; see p. 85.

Bloody flag
A red flag, otherwise known as the 'flag of defiance', used by European warships and corsairs in action in the 17th century.

'Blue Peter'
A blue flag with a white rectangle in the centre, now the letter P in the *International Code of Signals*. By itself it has the meaning: 'All persons should report on board as the vessel is about to proceed to sea'; see p. 84.

Bonaventure mizzen
The aftermost mast in the large four-masted ships of the 16th and early 17th centuries.

Breadth
The unit (along the hoist) of measurement for flags in the Royal Navy; see pp. 86-7.

Break out
To unfurl a flag that has been hoisted tied in such a way that a pull of the halyard causes it to open out; see Mead (Bibl. C18), pp. 51-3.

Broad pennant
A tapering flag, broader than a commissioning pennant; particularly for a commodore.

Budgee jack
The term used by Pepys for the privateer jack of 1694; see p. 25, and Perrin (Bibl. C23), pp. 69-70, 105, 125.

Bunting
The traditional all-wool cloth used for Royal Navy flags; see p. 85. To judge from the examples in the National Maritime Museum, the plain tabby weave of bunting altered relatively little from the 17th to the 20th century, but the earlier flags tend to be more loosely woven and their threads to be less uniform.

Burgee
The distinguishing flag of a yacht club, which in Great Britain is usually triangular. See p. 45; G. H. Burrows, 'Burgees', *Coat of Arms* 9 (1966-7), pp. 21-9; *MM* 54 (1968), p. 38; 55 (1969), pp. 16, 22. In the Royal Navy, a rectangular flag with a swallowtail.

Calico: A cotton fabric of Indian origin; see p. 85.

Canton
A heraldic term which, in describing a flag, refers to a rectangle in the upper hoist quarter; see p. 14. A canton in a flag may occupy a quarter of the area of a flag, or even more, but a heraldic canton occupies only a small part of the area of a shield of arms.

Cartel flag
A cartel ship is one involved in the exchange of prisoners. In 1780 a British ship with French prisoners on board used a combination of French and British flags as a sign of her status.

See D. Bonner Smith, 'The case of the *Sartine*', *MM* 21 (1935), pp. 305-22.

Church pennant
A special pennant hoisted to show that a ship's company are at religious service. The British church pennant has St George's cross at the hoist and the fly striped red over white over blue See *MM* 26 (1940), p. 244; A. R. McCracken, 'The Church pennant', *United States Naval Institute Proceedings* 56 (No. 330, 1930), pp. 717-9.

Colours
'Generally speaking a ship's suit of colours may be defined as the set of distinction flags appropriate to her status, comprising the ensign, jack, pennant, standard, command flag, and her company, corporation or club emblem' (Mead, Bibl. C18, p. 1). For Boteler in the 1630s, however, colours and ensigns were synonymous; see p. 96.

Command flag
See *Flag of Command*.

Commissioning pennant
See 'Masthead pennant'.

Commodore
A rank between captain and rear admiral. In the British navy the rank is a temporary one given to captains holding certain special appointments. A commodore flies a broad pennant. See p. 31; *MM* 4(1914), pp. 73-7. The senior master of a merchant shipping line or a yacht club may also be called 'commodore'.

Cornet/cornette
Usually in naval use a flag swallowtailed at the fly, particularly a signal flag. Now virtually obsolete.

Court martial
The Union Flag at the peak on a Royal Navy ship signifies that a court martial is in session.

Courtesy ensign
The merchant ensign of the country being visited by a ship of different nationality, or of the country to which she is bound; customarily flown at the fore or at a yard-arm. See p. 35; *Admiralty Manual* (Bibl. C1), p. 365; Mead (Bibl. C18), pp. 63-6. Courtesy ensigns are not normally worn by men of war.

Crown
Various types of crown are used in heraldry. See Boutell (Bibl. F2), pp. 183-9. See also *Finial*.

Deface
To add a badge to a flag, such as the British red and blue ensigns.

Dip
'To lower partially and temporarily' (*Admiralty Manual of Seamanship*). The dipping of a flag is a sign of respect. See *Queen's Regulations* (Bibl. C26), para. 1238.

Distinguishing flag
A flag used by an individual to denote his rank, command, office, or authority, indicating his presence in a ship or place.

Distress
A traditional sign of distress at sea is to turn the ensign upside down. See Fig. 93, and Mead (Bibl. C18), pp. 39-42.

Dress ship
To decorate a ship with various flags for a special occasion; see p. 95, and *Queen's Regulations* (Bibl. C26), para. 1240.

Ensign
A wide-ranging term, but most commonly applied to the national flag flown by ships at or near the stern; see index.

Ensign staff
A staff at the stern of the ship to carry the ensign.

Escutcheon
A heraldic term for a shield.

False colours
Flags, particularly national ensigns, flown by ships not entitled to them. By tradition at sea it is accepted that ships may use false colours to deceive an enemy as long as their true colours are hoisted before they open fire. See Perrin (Bibl. C23), pp. 198-9; Mead (Bibl. C18), pp. 47-9.

Fimbriation
A narrow border used in heraldry to prevent two metals (or, argent) or two colours (such as gules, azure) from coming into contact.

Finial
A decorative top to a flagstaff. In the Royal Navy a jackstaff is surmounted by a naval crown, an ensign staff by a royal crown.

Flag
An all-embracing general term; but also in naval usage specifically referring to a flag of command.

Flag of command
In naval usage the flag of an officer of the rank of rear admiral or above.

Flag of convenience
'A term applied to ships registered in certain small countries, notably Liberia and Panama, by owners who are not nationals of that country, thus flying flags which do not represent their true origin' (*Oxford Companion to Ships and the Sea*). The adoption of such a flag enables shipowners to employ cheap labour and avoid regulations applying to ships registered in the developed maritime countries. See R. Carlisle, *Sovereignty for Sale*, Annapolis 1981.

Flag officer
A naval officer of the rank of rear admiral or above.

Flagship
A ship flying the flag of a flag officer or the broad pennant of a commodore.

Fly (noun)
The part of a flag away from the hoist.

Fly (verb)
According to the *Admiralty Manual of Seamanship*, in the Royal Navy: 'Colours, standards and distinguishing flags are said to be worn by ships and individuals, and they may be said

to be flown in a ship or at a place. Other types of flag are only described as being 'flown' never as worn.' This distinction is not commonly observed in ordinary English, since 'wear' is obsolescent.

Foul anchor

An anchor entangled with its cable. See Perrin (Bibl. C23), pp. 82-3; A. P. Herbert, 'The foul anchor', *Coat of Arms* 6 (1960-1), pp. 101-3.

Gaff

A spar set diagonally on the after side of a mast. Ensigns are often flown from the peak of the gaff, that is, attached to a halyard passing through the outer end of the gaff of the mizzen mast, or of the main in a two-masted ship. See Figs. 47, 55.

Gules

The heraldic term for red.

Gyronny

A shield or a flag divided into sectors radiating from the centre.

Half-masting

Lowering a flag to a point some way below its normal position, usually as a sign of mourning; see *Queen's Regulations* (Bibl. C26), para. 1238; Mead (Bibl. C18), pp. 36-9.

Halyard

Flag halyards are ropes to which flags are attached by means of loops and toggles, or interlocking 'Inglefield clips'; the flag can then be hoisted or lowered by pulling on the halyard; see p. 88.

Hoist (noun)

The part of a flag next to the flagstaff.

Hoist (verb)

The normal word for putting up a flag at sea.

Homeward-bound pennant

The American term for the paying-off pennant.

House flag

The flag of a shipping company; see pp. 10, 36-9. The term is also sometimes used for the personal flag of a yacht owner.

Impale

A heraldic term for marshalling two coats of arms side by side in a shield or a flag.

Inglefield clip

The interlocking metal clips used in the Royal Navy and a few merchant shipping companies to attach flags to halyards. Patented by Lieut. Edward Fitzmaurice Inglefield, RN, in 1890 (Patent No. 14633: modified specification No. 16908, of 1893).

Jack

A small flag flown at the bows of a ship. The origin of the term is disputed. One theory derives it from the name of King James I, who introduced the first 'Union Jack' in 1606 (see p. 16), but a more probable one derives it from a supposed use of 'jack' as a general diminutive in 16th-century English; see *OED*.

Jackstaff

A staff for the jack, in the 17th century rigged on the bowsprit, now at the bows of a ship; see p. 17.

106 H.M. Submarine *Unison* on her return to England in 1943 after operations in the Mediterranean. The red bar in the upper fly corner of the 'Jolly Roger' denotes a warship sunk, the white bars merchant ships, and the broken bar a ship hit, the final fate of which was not known; the crossed guns and stars are for gun actions on the surface, the daggers for commando raids, and the torch for participation in Operation Torch (the invasion of North Africa)

Jolly Roger

A popular and literary term for the black flags with emblems of death supposedly used by pirates; see p. 46. The term dates from the early 18th-century.

Launching flags

See p. 22; *Queen's Regulations* (Bibl. C26), para. 1242; and C. H. Gaye-Hexham 'Launching flags in HM ships', *MM* 36 (1950), pp. 229-32.

Life-boat flags

See H. G. Carr, 'Flags of National Life-boat Societies', *MM* 25 (1939), pp. 133-50.

Livery colours

Colours used by armigerous families for the uniform of their retainers and for decoration; usually the principal metal and colour in their coat-of-arms.

Make her number

To hoist the group of signal flags that identify a ship in a signal code; see p. 83 and Mead (Bibl. C18), p. 70-9.

Masthead pennant

A long narrow pennant flown permanently by warships in commission, unless replaced by the command flag of a flag officer or a commodore's broad pennant. Also called 'commissioning pennant' or 'whip pennant'; the American term is 'commission pennant'. See index.

Merchant jack

A flag worn at the bows by a merchant ship. The British 'merchant jack' is the white-bordered Union, also called the 'pilot jack'. See pp. 34-5; Mead (Bibl. C17).

Metal

In heraldry the metals are or (gold/yellow) and argent (silver/white).

Mizzen

The aftermost mast of a three-masted ship.

Morse Code flags

The 1937 edition of the *Admiralty Manual of Seamanship* stipulated that Morse code flags should be blue, or white with a blue horizontal stripe.

Or

The heraldic term for yellow or gold.

Paying-off pennant

An elongated form of the commissioning pennant flown by a naval ship at the end of a commission; see *Admiralty Manual of Seamanship* (Bibl. C1), p. 364.

Peak

See *Gaff*.

Pennant

See index; Mead (Bibl. C18), pp. 84-6; Naval Historical Library, Search 185/39. The traditional British naval spelling is 'pendant' (pronounced 'pennant'), but since the Second World War 'pennant' has come to be widely used. Both spellings can be found in current Royal Navy publications. See also *Masthead pennant, Broad pennant*.

Pilot flag

The flag hoisted by a ship approaching port as a signal that she requires a pilot, normally nowadays the 'G' flag of the *International Code of Signals*.

Pilot jack

See *Merchant jack*.

Pratique

See *Quarantine flag*.

Private ship

In naval usage any ship in a naval fleet that is not a flagship.

Privateer

An armed ship with 'letters of marque' licensing it to take ships as prizes; see pp. 42-4.

Quarantine flag

A ship which has not yet received medical clearance on arrival flies a yellow flag (Q in the *International Code of Signals*) as a quarantine flag with the meaning 'My vessel is 'healthy' and I request free pratique', i.e. a certificate of good health. See p. 84.

Quartered

The four quarters of a quartered coat of arms or flag are numbered as shown.

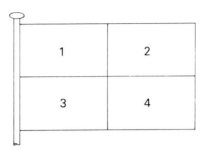

Queen's Colour

The Royal Navy 'Queen's Colour' (then 'King's Colour') was first presented in 1924. It is a white ensign charged with the royal cypher (EIIR) crowned and surrounded by the Garter. It is paraded on board H. M. Ships of the Fleet and on shore on occasions of royal ceremonial. See Barraclough and Crampton (Bibl. B5), p. 35; *Admiralty Manual of Seamanship* (Bibl. C1), p. 363; *Queen's Regulations* (Bibl. C26), para. 1231.

Repeating frigates

Frigates stationed outside or behind the main line in a fleet of sailing warships to relay signals to ships out of view of the flagship.

Revenue cutters

The patrol boats of the Customs and Excise, see p. 40.

Royal Mail pennant

The pennant flown by ships under contract to the Post Office carrying the Royal Mail; see p. 42.

Royal Standard

See 'Standard'.

Saltire

The heraldic term for a diagonal cross such as the cross of St Andrew (Plate I, no. 11).

Semaphore

A kind of telegraph involving the use of machines with moveable arms: see the series of articles by H.P. Mead 'The story of the Semaphore', *MM* 19 (1933); 20 (1934); 21 (1935); 24 (1938); 25 (1939); and G. Wilson, *The Old Telegraphs*, Chichester 1976. From around 1880, hand semaphore using flags was used in the Royal Navy to supplement semaphore machines. At first the design of semaphore flags was not fixed, but early in the 20th-century a flag divided diagonally red and yellow came to be standard. See *Admiralty Manual of Seamanship* (Bibl. C1), Fig. 13-7.

Semé

A heraldic term used when a coat of arms or a flag has an indefinite number of a charge strewn evenly over it.

Senior officer's pennant

A special pennant hoisted by the senior naval officer present in a group of naval ships, in the absence of a flag officer or commodore. The Royal Navy Senior officer's pennant from 1864 to 1950 was a white broad pennant with St George's cross, smaller than the pennant of a commodore. It was hoisted from the starboard upper yard arm and did not displace the masthead pennant. From 1950 NATO navies adopted the green-white-green 'starboard pennant' as a senior officer's pennant. See Perrin (Bibl. C23), pp. 107-9; *Queen's Regulations* (Bibl. C26), para. 1244.

Standard

To heralds, a standard is a long tapering flag, often incorporating badges, particularly used for pageantry. See Boutell (Bibl. F2), pp. 251-5. Standards of this sort were much used in the Tudor period. The habit of calling the banner of the Royal Arms the 'Royal Standard', though a heraldic solecism, dates back to the first half of the 17th century.

Streamer

The large pennants used particularly on royal ships and for celebration up to the 17th-century.

Strike

To take down a flag, particularly as a sign of deference or surrender.

Swallowtailed

Used of flags or pennants with an indentation, usually triangular, at the fly end (eg. Plate III, no. 28).

Toggle

A peg, normally of wood, which can be fitted into a loop to make a fastening.

Truck

'A circular or square cap of wood fixed on the head of a mast or flagstaff, usually with small holes or sheaves for halyards' (*OED*).

Union Jack

The small version of the Union Flag worn at the bows of Royal Navy ships; see index. Compare *Jack*. In the United States the starry jack (the canton of the 'Stars and Stripes' used alone) is known in the Navy as the 'Union Jack'.

Vane

The short pennants used by merchant ships, and by warships at masts where no proper pennant was flying, particularly in the 17th and 18th centuries. They were of various shapes and sometimes stiffened on a framework. See p. 27.

Vexillology

The study of flags. The term was coined in 1957 (from the Latin *vexillum*, a standard).

Wear

See *Fly* (vb).

Wheft

The meaning of this term has varied over the years. Mainwaring's *Seaman's Dictionary*, first published in 1644, says: 'Wafts are used for signes to have the boate come aboord (which is Coate, Gowne or the like hung-up in the Shrowdes); also it is a common signe of some extremity, a ship doth hang a wafte upon the maine-stay either that it has sprung a-leake or is in some distresse'. Lord Howe's Signal Book of 1776 (NMM, MS HOL/21, p. 2) has 'A wheft . . . is to be made by stopping the head part of the flag only and leaving the fly loose'. See Mead (Bibl. C18), pp. 86-9.

Whip pennant

See *Masthead pennant*.

Classified Bibliography

For ease of reference the bibliography has been classified into sections, as follows:

A Flag books and flag plates to 1860, arranged by date

B Flag books and general works from 1860 to the present, arranged alphabetically

C Works on British and Irish flags

D Works on the flags of some foreign nations, arranged alphabetically by country

E Works on shipping company house flags

F Miscellaneous

British government (Admiralty etc.) and other official publications are entered alphabetically by title.

The bibliography includes the general works that have been found most useful in compiling this book, together with a number of works that may help the reader who wants to follow up particular subjects. (For references on points of detail, the reader should consult the notes.) It is biased towards British sources and with occasional exceptions is limited to works available in the National Maritime Museum, the Naval Historical (formerly Admiralty) Library (Empress State Building, London SW6), or the British Library. A more comprehensive listing of books on flags is Whitney Smith's *Bibliography of the Flags of Foreign Nations*, of which a new edition is in preparation.

Works of particular usefulness in the field covered by this book are marked with an asterisk.

A: Flag books and flag plates to 1860

Note: Flag books and flag plates before the middle of the 19th century have to be treated sceptically. Most are derivative, slipshod and frequently out of date. Once engraved, a plate of flags was liable to be re-used for many years with only token updatings: for instance, the arms of King William III, who died in 1702, are still shown as the royal arms of Great Britain in Continental flag plates of more than fifty years later. In the 18th and 19th centuries flag plates were issued separately, bound up with encyclopaedias or atlases, or chopped up and made into pocket flag books. The National Maritime Museum also has early 19th-century flag plates printed on silk.

In 1875 appeared the first edition of the British Admiralty's *Drawings of the Flags in Use at the Present Time by various Nations* (Bibl. B9). There have been several editions since, with addenda sheets between editions to keep them up to date. Similar publications have been issued by the naval authorities of France, Germany and the United States. These works are much more reliable than earlier flag books. In recent years there has grown up a serious scholarly study of flags with a network of contacts between flag experts across the world. The Flag Research Center, 3 Edgehill Road, Winchester, Massachusetts, U.S.A., and other similar groups in other countries, have accumulated important bodies of information on flags past and present, and their publications often have an authority formerly confined to official government publications. In Great Britain the Flag Institute, currently based at 10 Vicarage Road, Chester, has probably the best specialized library in Great Britain of modern material on flag history, and publishes a periodical newsletter *Flagmaster*; the addresses of these and some other vexillological organizations can be currently obtained through the Heraldry Society, 45 Museum Street, London WC1. The Heraldry Society's library also holds a number of vexillological periodicals.

For the detailed bibliography of early flag books see Chapin (Bibl. B7); Sierksma (Bibl. A3).

A1
The Book of the Knowledge of all the Kingdoms, Lands and Lordships that are in the World: a manuscript treatise by a 14th-century Spanish Franciscan; Hakluyt Society, New Series No. 29, 1912. See S. Herreros Agui, 'El Libro del Conocimiento de todos los Reynos', *Banderas* 1-2 (1979), pp. 26-30; G. Pasch in *Vexillologia* 2, nos. 1-2 (1969), pp. 8-32.

A2
Cleirac, E., *Les Us et Coutumes de la Mer*, Rouen 1647, and other editions. This contains an important discussion of flags, first published in 1636, but it is not illustrated.

A3
Flags of the World 1669-70: a manuscript edited in facsimile by Kl. Sierksma, Amsterdam 1966.

A4
Les pavillons et les étendars des mers suivant la diversitté des nations: a manuscript probably made in Toulon, *c.* 1670; see L. Mühlemann, 'Les Pavillons des nations maritimes au XVIIe siècle d'après le manuscrit de J. Moutton', *Recueil du 4e congrès international de vexillologie*, Turin 1971.

107 Title page of the flag book of Paulus Van der Dussen, c 1690[1] (Bibl. A 8)

108 From an English signal book of 1711 (Bibl. A 17)

A5

Insignia Navalia: a manuscript by Lieutenant John Graydon, dated 1686, in the Pepys Library, Magdalene College, Cambridge, MS. 1608; see Wilson (Bibl. B35); Knighton (Bibl. F10).

A6

Two pages of flag drawings in a manuscript of 1685-6 by William Downman, in the manuscript collection of the National Maritime Museum; ref. NVT/8. Plate IV.

A7

Desroches, *Dictionnaire des termes propres de marine,* Paris 1687.

A8

Vlagge-Boeck van den Heer Paulus van der Dussen, Capitein: a Dutch manuscript flag book of *c.* 1690 in the manuscript collection of the National Maritime Museum; ref. SIG/C/12. See K1. Sierksma in *Spiegel Historiael* 14 (1979), pp. 663-8. Figs. 27, 106.

*A9

Allard, C., *Nieuwe Hollandse Scheeps-bouw,* Amsterdam 1694, and later, expanded, editions: the library of the National Maritime Museum contains editions dated 1695 and 1705, and an

edition issued by J. Oosterwyk in Amsterdam in 1716. This is the most thorough and influential flag book of the period. According to Klaes Sierksma (personal communication) there is evidence of an earlier edition, *c*1685; see *MM* 9 (1923), pp. 217, 379. Figs. 20, 72, 86.

A10

A series of twelve sumptuous flag plates published by P. Mortier of Amsterdam in 1700-1. These are often found bound up with the *Neptune Franç*ois, an atlas first published in 1693. They are based on Allard (Bibl. A9). Figs. 74, 77, 78, 83.

A11

A General View of the Flags which most Nations bear at Sea: a flag plate printed by B. Lens, *c.* 1700. Plate VI.

A12

Hesman, G., a Friesian manuscript flag book *c.* 1700, edited by Kl. Sierksma and J.C. Terluin, Ljouwert 1975.

A13

Beaumont. J., *The Present State of the Universe,* London 3rd ed., 1702.

A14

De Ge-öfnete See-Hafen, Hamburg (Benjamin Schiller) 1702.

A15

A. Justice, *A General Treatise of the Dominion and Laws of the Sea*, London 1705. The flag plates are related to Bibl. A11.

A16

Table des pavillons quil'on arbore dans toutes les Parties du Monde Connu, Cousernant la Marinne: a flag plate produced by C. Danckerts, *c.* 1710; see W. Smith '250 years of Dutch Flag Charts', *FB* 4 (1964-5), pp. 62-70.

A17

Drawings of flags in an English manuscript signal book, dated 1711, in the manuscript collection of the National Maritime Museum; ref. SIG/B/1. Figs. 63, 91, 107.

A18

Tableau des Pavillons que les Vaisseaux de toutes les Nations arborent sur les Mers: a flag plate published by M. Seutter, 1712.

A19

L'Art de Batir les Vaisseaux, Amsterdam 1719.

A20

La Connoissance des Pavillons ou Bannières que la plupart des Nations arborent en mer, published by J. van den Kieboom, The Hague 1737. Fig. 61.

A21

Millan, J., *Signals for the Royal Navy*, London 1746-8.

A22

Drawings of flags in an English manuscript signal book of *c.* 1756 in the manuscript collection of the National Maritime Museum; ref. SIG/B/6. Fig. 10.

A23

Bellin, J.N., *Tableau des Pavillons que la Pluspart des Nations arborent a la mer*, Paris 1756.

A24

Plates of flags under the heading *Marine* in Vol. 7 of the *Recueil de Planches* of Diderot's *Encyclopédie ou Dictionnaire raisonné des sciences des arts et des métiers*, Paris 1769.

A25

Bowles, C., *Bowles's Universal Display of the Naval Flags of all Nations in the World*, London 1783, and later editions.

A26

'Royal and Signal Colours': a collection of manuscript material and official papers on flags from the 18th and 19th centuries in the Naval Historical Library; ref. De 010; see Mead (Bibl. B21).

A27

The Maritime Flags of all Nations, published by W. Heather, London 1800, and later editions; also published as a single plate in Heather's *Marine Atlas*.

A28

Plates descriptive of the Maritime Flags of all Nations, published by J.W. Norie, London 1819, and later editions. Norie took over Heather's business in 1812. Fig. 50.

A29

The Maritime Flags of all Nations, published by R.H. Laurie, London 1821, and later editions. Plate VIII.

A30

A Display of the Naval Flags of all Nations, printed by M. Fisher, London 1823, and later editions.

A31

Drawings of the National Flags of the Several Maritime Powers: a manuscript of *c.* 1830 in the Naval Historical Library; ref. De 03.

A32

Maritime Flags of all Nations, published by Blachford and Imray, London *c.* 1840.

A33

An English manuscript flag book dated 1845 in the Naval Historical Library; ref. De 04.

*A34

Le Gras, A., *Album des pavillons, guidons, flammes de toutes les puissances maritimes*, Paris 1858.

B: Flag books and general works from 1860

B1

Album des pavillons nationaux et des marques distinctives, Service hydrographique de la Marine, France, 1979, and previous editions.

*B2

Archibald, E.H.H., *Dictionary of Sea Painters*, Woodbridge 1980, pp. 18-29.

B3

Barraclough, E.M.C., 'Ensigns', *Motor Boat and Yachting*, 23 April 1965, pp. 58-61.

B4

Barraclough, E.M.C., 'Three historic flags', *FB* 10 (1981), pp. 69-80.

*B5

Barraclough, E.M.C., & Crampton W.G., *Flags of the World*, London 1981, and previous editions (edited successively by F.E. Hulme, W.J. Gordon, V. Wheeler-Holohan, and H.G. Carr).

B6

Campbell, G., & Evans, I.O., *The Book of Flags*, London 1974, and previous editions.

B7

Chapin, H.M., 'Seventeenth century flag books', *American Book Collector* 3 (1933), pp. 332-4, and 4 (1933), pp. 38-42.

B8

Flaggenbuch, Oberkommando der Marine, Germany, 1893 and later editions.

*B9

Flags of All Nations (formerly *Drawings of the Flags in use at the present time by Various Nations*), Admiralty, U.K. (now Ministry of Defence, Navy, ref. BR 20), 1875, 1889, 1907, 1916, 1930, 1955-58, with amendments. The Admiralty files at the Public Record Office at Kew include several batches of correspondence between 1873 and 1930 on the revisions and amendments to the series of Flag Books; see the Class List (typescript at Kew) to ADM 116, Part I, Volume II, section 20, 'Flags and Crests'. Figs. 51, 52.

B10

Flags of Maritime Nations, Bureau of Navigation, Navy Dept., U.S.A., 1868 and later editions (more recent editions published by the Hydrographic Office).

B11

Gritzner, A.M., *Flaggen*, vol. 1, part vi, of Siebmacher's *Wappenbuch*, Nuremberg 1878.

B12

Harring, R.M., Manuscript notes on flags, with collection of transcripts and cuttings, NMM, MS. REC/47/1-3.

B13

Heraldry Society, Flag Section, *Dictionary of Flag Terminology*, London 1969.

B14

Hill, C., Manuscript notes on flags, particularly the use of red and black flags, Naval Historical Library, ref. De 06.

B15

Horstmann, H., *Vor- und Frühgeschichte des europaischen Flaggenwesens*, Bremen 1971.

B16

Hounsell, G.C., *Flags and Signals of all Nations*; London undated, *c*.1873 (the precursor of the British Admiralty's series of flag books, Bibl. B9).

B17

King C., 'Essentials of Sea Armory', *The Studio* 85 (1923), pp. 89-95.

***B18**

King, C., 'Flags in marine art', *MM* 22 (1936), pp. 133-60.

B19

Laughton, J.K., 'The heraldry of the sea', *Journal of the RUSI*, 23 (1879), pp. 116-48.

B20

Lyman, J., 'Maritime law and flag usage', *Proceedings of the 6th International Congress of Vexillology*, Netherlands 1975, pp. 33-45.

B21

Mead, H.P., 'Royal and Signal colours', *MM* 37 (1951), pp. 143-64; 38 (1952) pp. 53-65

B22

Neubecker, O., *Fahnen und Flaggen*, Leipzig 1939.

B23

Pasch, G., 'Les drapeaux des cartes-portolans', *Vexillologia*, vol. 3, no. 2 (1973), pp. 52-62; vol. 1, nos. 2-3 (1967), pp. 38-60; vol. 2, nos 1-2 (1969), pp. 8-32.

B24

Pasch, G., 'Flags over the Americas', *FB* 18 (1979), pp. 142-84.

B25

Pedersen, C., *The International Flag Book*, London 1971.

B26

Purves, A.A., *Flags for Ship Modellers and Marine Artists* (London 1950; repr. 1983).

***B27**

Purves, A.A., 'Flags for the ship modeller', *Model Shipwright*, vol. 1, no. 1 (1972), pp. 75-7; vol. 1, no. 2 (1972), pp. 175-8; vol. 1, no. 3 (1973), pp. 225-8; vol. 1, no. 4 (1973), pp. 348-52; vol. 2 no. 1 (1973), pp. 41-5; vol. 2, no. 4 (1974), pp. 388-90; no. 10 (1974), pp. 141-4; no. 13 (1975), pp. 40-1; no. 27 (1979), pp. 48-51; no. 29 (1979), pp. 40-4.

B28

Rijksmuseum, Amsterdam, *Vlaggen, vaandels & standaarden*, by M. van den Brandhof, Amsterdam 1977.

***B29**

Siegel, R., *Die Flagge*, Berlin 1912.

B30

Sierksma, Kl., *L'Histoire fixée en drapeaux* (a portfolio of flag charts), Bussum 1975.

B31

Sierksma, Kl., *Vlaggen; Symbolie, traditie, protocol*, Bussum 1963.

***B32**

Smith, W., *Bibliography of the Flags of Foreign Nations*, Boston 1965.

B33

Smith, W., 'Bibliography: vexillological serials', *FB* 16 (1977), pp. 75-83.

***B34**

Smith, W., *Flags through the Ages and across the World*, Maidenhead etc., 1975.

B35

Steenbergen, *Vlaggen van alle natien*, Amsterdam 1862.

B36

Wilson,T. H., 'Some manuscripts of flag interest in the Pepys Library, Magdalene College, Cambridge', *Proceedings of the 8th International Congress of Vexillology, Vienna 1979* (not yet published).

B37

Wise, T., *Military Flags of the World*, Poole 1977.

B38

Woods, D.L., 'The Evolution of Visual Signals on Land and Sea', Ph. D. thesis, Ohio State University, 1976 (copy in NMM Library).

C: Works on British and Irish flags

C1

Admiralty Manual of Seamanship, I, Admiralty, U.K. (now Ministry of Defence, Navy, ref. BR 67(1)), 1972, and earlier editions.

C2

Barraclough, E.M.C., 'The British sailor and his flags', *FB* 11 (1972), pp. 266-74.

C3

Barraclough, E.M.C., *Yacht Flags and Ensigns*, London 1951.

C4

Barraclough, E.M.C., and Wilson, J., 'The Union Flag of Britain', *Coat of Arms*, New Series, vol. 4, no. 120 (1981-2), pp. 430-3; vol. 5, no. 121 (1982), pp. 2-8.

C5

Bellew, G., 'An examination of the flags and heraldry on the contemporary picture of the *Mary Rose*', *Coat of Arms*, New Series, vol. 5, no. 122 (1982), pp. 47-53.

C6

Blomfield, R.M., 'British naval flags of command', *MM* 6 (1920), pp. 207-12.

C7

Boteler, N., *Dialogues*, ed. W.G. Perrin, NRS 65, 1929 (See Appendix B).

*C8

Corbett, J., *Fighting Instructions 1530-1816*, NRS 29, 1905.

*C9

Corbett, J., *Signals and Instructions 1776-94*, NRS 35, 1908.

C10

Harvey, C., *The Scottish Flags*, Glasgow 1914.

C11

Hayes-McCoy, G.A., *A History of Irish Flags*, Dublin 1979.

C12

Holland, L.E., 'The development of signalling in the Royal Navy', *MM* 39 (1953), pp. 5-26.

C13

Irving, J., *Manual of Flag Etiquette*, London 1934.

C14

King, C., *The History of British Flags*, London 1914.

*C15

King, C., 'The King's flags and some others', *MM* 38 (1952), pp. 84-105.

C16

MacMillan, W., and Stewart, J., *The Story of the Scottish Flag*, Glasgow 1925.

C17

Mead, H.P., 'The British merchant jack', *MM* 21 (1935), pp. 395-40.

*C18

Mead, H.P., *Sea Flags: Their General Use*, Glasgow 1938.

C19

Mead, H.P., *Trafalgar Signals*, London 1936.

C20

Mead, H.P. & 'Buccaneer', 'Naval signalling', *Brassey's Annual* 1953, pp. 177-200.

C21

Naval Historical Library, Searches, no. 185 (a collection of correspondence and information on flag affairs).

C22

Peacock, A., 'The Queen's sea flags', *MM* 43 (1957), pp. 267-80.

*C23

Perrin, W.G., *British Flags*, Cambridge 1922.

C24

Perrin, W.G., 'British naval ensigns', *MM* 1 (1911), pp. 167 bis – 172 bis.

C25

Purves, A.A., 'The functions of the Union Flag', *MM* 37 (1951), pp. 231-6.

*C26

Queen's Regulations for the Royal Navy (formerly *Queen's/King's Regulations and Admiralty Instructions*), Ministry of Defence, Navy, U.K., ref. BR 31, in progress (See Appendix D for the first edition, 1731).

C27

Snider, G.H.J., *The glorious Shannon's Old Blue Duster and other Faded Flags of Fadeless Fame*, Toronto 1923.

C28

Stewart, C., *Yacht Club Burgees*, Southampton 1957.

C29

Visual Signalling and Equipment Handbook, Admiralty, U.K. (ref. BR 1971), 1953.

D: Works on the sea flags of other nations

Austria

D1

Baumgartner, L., 'Die Entwicklung der österreichischen Marine-flagge', *Militaria Austriaca* 1977, pp. 29-40.

D2

Benson, G.S., 'Command flags of Austria-Hungary 1780-1915' *FB* 6 (1967), pp. 156-66.

Belgium

D3

Boudin, H.R., & Baert, R., *Bibliographie du drapeau belge*, Brussels 1975; and in *Vexilla Belgica* 1 (1977).

D4

Gaye-Hexham, C.H., 'Maritime flags of Belgium', *Nautical Magazine* 164 (1950), pp. 256-7.

Canada

D5

Spence, D.R., 'An outline history of Canada's flags', *FB* 20 (1980), pp. 319-27.

Denmark

D6

Achen, S.T., 'Dannebrog: the national flag of Denmark', *FB* 8 (1969), pp. 146-65.

France

D7

Bouillé, L. de, *Les Drapeaux français*, 2nd ed., Paris 1875.

D8

Chartrand, R., 'Flags of New France', *FB* 15 (1976), pp. 13-21.

D9

Desjardins, G., *Recherches sur les drapeaux français*, Paris 1874.

D10

King, C., 'Distinction marks in French command flags', *MM* 8 (1922), pp. 9-15.

D11

King, C., 'The French ensign and the white colours', *MM* 25 (1939), pp. 286-95.

D12

King, C., 'The French flags of 1790', *MM* 10 (1924), pp. 147-55.

D13

King, C., 'Sea flags of France', *Yachting Monthly* 31 (1920-21), pp. 391-8; 32 (1921-2), pp. 3-10; 79-87.

D14

Lux-Wurm, P.C., 'The development and meanings of white as a French national colour', *FB* 12 (1973), pp. 129-35.

D15

Pasch, G., 'Drapeaux et pavillons des villes maritimes françaises', *Neptunia* 61 (1961), pp. 10-13; 63 (1961), pp. 15-18; 65 (1962), pp. 22-4; 68 (1962), pp. 15-18.

D16

Philippe, L., 'The French tricolour and its influence on flags throughout the world', *FB* 10 (1971), pp. 55-67.

Germany

D17

Davis, B.L., *Flags and Standards of the Third Reich*, London 1975.

D18

Mattern, G., & Neubecker, O., 'Beitrag zur Geschichte und Flagge deutschen Länder: 3: Küstenländer', *Jahrbuch des heraldischen Vereins 'zum Kleeblat'*, Hanover, 16-17 (1978-9), pp. 71-106.

D19

Witthöft, H.J., *Lexikon zur deutschen Marinegeschichte*, Herford 1977-8, I, pp. 88-90.

Italy

D20

Biasi, M., *Il Gonfalone di San Marco*, Venice 1981.

D21

Ziggioto, A. 'Le bandiere degli stati italiani', *Armi Antiche* (Bollettino dell 'Accademia di San Marciano, Turin), 1967, pp. 179-98; 1968, pp. 113-32; 1969, pp. 129-42; 1970, pp. 93-128; Numero speciale per il 4° Congresso Internazionale di Vessillologia, 1971, pp. 45-118; supplements in *Vexilla Italica*, 1975-8.

D22

Ziggioto, A., 'Flags of Italy', *FB* 6 (1966-7), pp. 141-50; 7 (1968), pp. 56-64; 96-107; 9 (1970), pp. 10-20; 99-106; 120-8.

D22a

Ziggioto, A., 'Le bandiere delle città medievali e quelle degli stati pre-unitari', in G. Bascapé and M. del Piazzo, *Insegne e Simboli: Araldica pubblica e privata medievale e moderna*, Rome 1983, pp. 447-81.

The Netherlands

D23

Cannenburg, W.V., 'De Prinsenvlag', *Gedenkboek Prins Willem van Oranje*, Haarlem 1933, pp. 401-8.

D24

Dulm, J.F. van, 'Introduction to the signal flags of the Netherlands Navy', *Petit recueil du rencontre des amis européens de la bannistique*, Temse 1969.

D25

Jonge, J.C. de, *Over den oorsprong der nederlandsche vlag*, The Hague & Amsterdam 1831.

D26

Jonker, L., *Wat is de oorsprong van onze vlag?*, Middelburg 1937.

D27

Laars, T. van der, *Wapens, vlaggen en zegels van Nederland*, Amsterdam 1913.

D28

Nederlandsch Historisch Scheepvaart Museum, *Catalogus der bibliotheek*, Amsterdam 1960.

D29

Pama, C., *Lions and Virgins*, Cape Town and Pretoria 1965.

D30

Pama, C., *Het wapen der Nederlanden*, The Hague 1942.

D31

Sierksma, Kl., *Nederlands vlaggenboek*, Utrecht 1962.

D32

Treu, H.A., 'De koninklijke hollandse vlag van 1806-1810' *Marineblad* 4 (1970), pp. 483-96.

D33

Treu, H.A., *De nederlandse vlag en de nederlandse koninklijke vlaggen*, The Hague 1971.

D34

Waard, C. de, *De nederlandse vlag*, Groningen 1900.

D35

Wie is wat, wat is wie?, an undated, current leaflet of the flags and badges of the Royal Netherlands Navy.

Portugal

D36

Parmelee, K.W., 'The flag of Portugal in history and legend', *Romanic Review* 9 (1918), pp. 291-303.

D37

Pye, R.F., 'Development of the arms of Portugal in fact and legend', *Coat of Arms* 5 (1958-9), pp. 187-90; 252-4.

D38

Santos Ferreira, G.L., *Bandeiras navaes portuguesas*, Lisbon 1910.

Spain

D39

Almirall Fusté, J., *Las banderas españolas de 1704 a 1977*, Barcelona 1978.

D40

Fernandez Duro, C., *Disquisiciones nauticas*, I, Madrid 1876; VI, Madrid 1881.

D41

Fernandez Duro, C., *Tradiciones infundadas*, Madrid 1888.

D42

Fernandez Espeso, C., 'The development on the concept of a national flag in Spain', *FB* 10 (1971), pp. 244-9.

D43

Fernandez Gaytan, J., 'El pabellon nacional', *Revista General de Marina* 187 (1974), pp. 131-40; 188 (1975), pp. 70-2.

D44

Fernandez Gaytan, J., 'Las banderas de la armada española', *Revista General de Marina* 204 (1983), pp. 203-17.

D45

Guillen Tato, J. F., *Historia maritima española*, Madrid 1961.

D46

Herreros Agüi, S., *Bibliografia sobre banderas españolas*, Madrid 1978 (supplements in *Banderas, Boletin de la Sociedad española de vexilologia*).

D47

King, C., 'The flags of Spain', *Connoisseur* 98 (1938), pp. 247-52.

D48

'New flags: Spanish state', *FB* 21 (1982), pp. 43-56.

D49

Van Ham, W.A., 'The cross of Burgundy: a symbol through five ages', *Proceedings of the 6th International Congress of Vexillology*, Netherlands 1975, pp. 87-98.

D50

Vicente Cascante, I., *Heraldica general y fuentes de las armas de España*, Barcelona etc., 1956.

Sweden

D51

Åberg, A., 'The national flags of Sweden', *FB* 18 (1979), pp. 128-36.

United States of America

D52

Chapin, H.M., *The Artistic Motives in the United States Flag*, Providence 1930.

D53

Chapin, H.M., *The New England Flag*, Providence 1930.

D54

Chapin, H.M., *Roger Williams and the King's Colors*, Providence 1928.

D55

Cooper, G.R., *Thirteen Star Flags: Keys to Identification*, Smithsonian Studies in History and Technology 21, Washington D.C. 1973.

D56

Flags, Pennants and Colors, Naval Telecommunications Dept., U.S.A., ref. NTP 13, 1977.

*D57

Furlong, R., & McCandless, B., *So Proudly We Hail*, Washington D.C. 1981.

*D58

Lyman, J., 'Flags of rank, command and dignity in the United States Navy 1777-1977', *FB* 19 (1980), pp. 198-205.

D59

Mastai, B., & Mastai, M.L. d'O., *The Stars and the Stripes*, New York 1973.

D60

Preble, G.H., *Origin and History of the American Flag*, 2nd ed., Philadelphia 1917.

D61

Quaife, M.M., & al., *The History of the United States Flag*, New York 1961.

D62

Rankin, H.F., 'The Naval flag of the American Revolution', *William & Mary Quarterly*, 3rd Series, 11 (1954), pp. 339-53.

D63

Richardson, E.W., *Standards & Colors of the American Revolution*, Philadelphia 1982.

D64

Schermerhorn, F.E., *American and French Flags of the Revolution 1775-83*, Philadelphia 1948.

*D65

Smith, W., *The Flag Book of the United States*, second edition, New York 1975.

Yugoslavia

D66

Pasch, G., 'Pavillons des villes de la côte Dalmate au moyen âge', *Neptunia* 77 (1965), pp. 2-6.

E: Works on Shipping company house flags

E1

Bates, L.M., 'House flags on London River', *PLA Monthly*, May 1939, pp. 167-70; June 1939, pp. 213-15.

E2

Lloyds Book of House Flags and Funnels, London 1904.

E3

Lloyds Code of Distinguishing Flags of the Steamship Owners of the United Kingdom, London 1882.

*E4

Loughran, J.L., *A Survey of Mercantile House Flags and Funnels*, Wolverhampton 1979.

E5

Merchant Marine House Flags and Stack Insignia, Hydrographic Office, U.S.A., 1961.

E6

Stewart, C.F., *Flags, Funnels and Hull Colours*, London 1953.

E7
Styring, J.S., *Brown's Flags and Funnels of British and Foreign Steamship Companies*, Glasgow 1971.

E8
Styring, J.S., 'A study in house flags', *Nautical Magazine* 112 (1924), pp. 6-10; 108-13; 234-7; 328-31; 416-16; 506-11; and 113 (1925), pp. 43-7; 104-5.

*E9
Styring, J.S., Manuscript card index of house flags, NMM.

E10
Wardle, A.C., 'Liverpool merchant signals and house flags', *MM* 34 (1948), pp. 161-8.

E11
Wedge, F.J.N., *Brown's Flags and Funnels of British and Foreign Steamship Companies*, Glasgow 1926.

F: Miscellaneous

F1
Bol, L.J., *Die holländische Marinemalerei des 17. Jahrhunderts*, Brunswick 1973.

F2
Boutell, C., *Boutell's Heraldry*, ed. J.P. Brooke-Little, London 1978.

F3
Boymans-van Beuningen Museum, Rotterdam, *The Willem Van de Velde Drawings in the Boymans-van Beuningen Museum*, Rotterdam 1979.

F4
British Library, *Sir Francis Drake*, exhibition catalogue 1977.

F5
British Museum, *Catalogue of British Drawings*, I, by E. Croft-Murray & P. Hulton, London 1960.

F6
Callender, G.A.R., *The Portrait of Peter Pett and the 'Sovereign of the Seas'*, Society for Nautical Research, Newport 1930.

*F7
Clowes, W.L., *The Royal Navy: a History*, London 1897-1903.

F8
Hakluyt, R., *Principal Navigations*, Glasgow 1903-5.

F9
Howard, G., *Sailing Ships of War*, Greenwich 1979.

F10
Knighton, C.S., *Catalogue of the Pepys Library at Magdalene College, Cambridge*, V, part ii, *Manuscripts, modern*, Woodbridge & Totown, N.J., 1981.

F11
Lewis, M.A., *England's Sea Officers*, London 1939.

F12
Louda, J., *European Civic Coats of Arms*, London 1966.

F13
National Maritime Museum, *The Art of the Van de Veldes*, exhibition catalogue 1982.

*F14
National Maritime Museum, *A Catalogue of the Van de Velde drawings in the NMM*, by M.S. Robinson, 1958-74

F15
Oppenheim, M., *A history of the Administration of the Royal Navy*, London & New York 1896.

F16
Pepys, S., *Diary*, ed. R.C. Latham & W. Matthews, London 1970-83.

F17
Pinches, J.H., & Pinches, R.V., *The Royal Heraldry of England*, London 1974.

F18
Preston, R., *The Seventeenth Century Marine Painters of the Netherlands*, Leigh on Sea 1974.

F19
Smyth, W.H., *Sailor's Word Book*, London 1867.

F20
Tunstall, B., *British and French Naval Tactics 1650-1815*, typescript, NMM, MS. 70 132.

Classified Bibliography: Addenda

B: Flag books and general works from 1860

B9
Flags of All Nations (note now a 1987 edition).

Crampton, William, *The World of Flags: a Pictorial History*, London 1990.

Real, Maria Eloisa Alvarez del, *Banderas y Escudos del Mundo*, Panama 1986.

Lyman, Dr John, 'Maritime Law and Flag Usage', *FB* 179 (1998).

C: Works on British and Irish flags

Kent, Barrie *Signal! A history of signalling in the Royal Navy*, Clanfield 1993.

D: Works on the sea flags of other nations

Spain

Perez, Jose Luis Calvo and Gonzalez, Luis Gravalos, *Banderas de Espana*, Madrid 1983.

United State of America

Madaus, H Michael, 'Rebel flags afloat: a survey of the surviving flags of the Confederate States Navy, Revenue Service and Merchant Marine', *FB* 115 (1986).

Gamez, John H, 'Flags and Signals of the Texas Navy', *FB* 162 (1995).

E: Works on Shipping company house flags

An Illustrated Register of Thames Tugs 1933-35 (shows funnel designs including house flags). In the manuscript collection of the National Maritime Museum; ref.MS94/002.

An Illustrated List of Flags and Insignia ca.1950's (shows house flags of Thames craft). In the manuscript collection of the National Maritime Museum; ref. MS94/003.

F: Miscellaneous

Tomlinson, Barbara, 'Chinese Flags in the Collections of the National Maritime Museum', *FB* 140 (1991).

Index

Adams, John   49
Admiral of the Fleet   18, 21, 27, 31, 95, 98, 99
Admiral of the Red   31, 99
Admiralty
– British   22, 34-5, 44, 81-2, 89, 97, 98 and see 'Lord High Admiral'
– Admiralty Library see 'Naval Historical Library'
– Dutch   56-7
Admiralty Flag – see 'Lord High Admiral'
Admiralty Manual of Seamanship   32, 82, 109, 110, 111, 116
Alert, HMS   48-9 (Fig 65)
Alfred   38 (Fig 42)
Allard, Carel   24 (Fig 20), 53 (Fig 72), 59, 64 (Fig 86), 114
Alliance   50, 104 (note 99)
America, Flags of   35, 47-52, Plate XIV, numbers 1-7
L'Amérique   89-90 (Fig 98)
Amsterdam   36, 53, 56-8 (Fig 77), 85, 87, 90, 105 (notes 114-5)
Anchor Flag – See 'Lord High Admiral'
'Anchor and Hope'   22
'Ancient'   14
Anne, Queen of Great Britain – Royal Standards of: Plate I, numbers 2, 4
Anthony Anthony Roll   100 (notes 4, 7)
Aragon   53, 56
Ark Royal   15, 101 (note 18)
Armada   12, 14, 54, 85; Plate V
Armillary sphere   55 (Fig 74)
Audley, Thomas   13, 77
Austria   53, 117

Badges   12, 18, 31, 85, 93-4, 100 (note 3), 102 (note 40), 108
Baffin, William   101 (note 27)
Banner   108
– Royal Banner   10, and see 'Standard'

– Armorial   12, 85, 100 (note 16); Plate XII
Barbary corsairs   46 (Fig 61)
Barcelona: Plate IX
Barge flags: 108
Barlow, Edward   22, 36 (Fig 38), 102 (notes 38, 41, 44)
Barraclough, EMC   8, 32, 115
Batavian Republic   60 (Fig 81), 89; Plate XV, number 10
Beauchamp Pageants   100 (notes 3, 5)
Beaumont, J   114
Bellin, J   115
Benin   89-90 (Fig 100)
Bewpers   85, 106-7 (note 148), 108
Bidston Hill   37-8 (Fig 41), 103 (note 73)
Blachford and Imray   115
Black Flag   116, and see 'Jolly Roger'
Blake, Robert   77
'Bloody Flag'   46, 61, 77, 79, 108, 116; Plate III, number 27
Blue Peter   84, 108
Boat flags   32, 98
Bodleian Library   101 (note 36), 106 (note 133)
Boer War   89
Bolt, DR   89
Bombay Marine   103 (note 72)
Bonaventure mizzen   14, 108
Bonhomme Richard   104 (note 99)
Borer, HMS   49 (Fig 67), 51
Boteler, Nathaniel   18, 19, 40, 95-6
Bowles, C   115
Boymans-van Beuningen Museum   58, 102 (note 44), 105 (note 116)
Brabant   53
'Breadth'   86-8, 107 (note 162), 108
'Break out'   108
Britannia
– HMS   31
– Royal Yacht (1893)   45 (Fig 59), 92
– Royal Yacht (1953)   32 (Fig 32), 89, 102 (note 42)
British Code List   84
'British Flag'   16, 96, and see 'Union Jack'

Brocklebank   39
Brown, John   12, 85, 93
Brunswick, HMS   87, 89
Buckingham, HMS   23 (Fig 18)
Buckland Abbey   92, 103 (note 63), 107 (note 150)
Buckram   106-7 (note 148)
Budgee jack   108 and see 'Privateer jack'
Budgee pennant   25 (Fig 23)
Bunting   85, 108
Burgee   44-5 (Fig 58), 104 (note 84), 108
Burgundy   53; Plate XIV, number 8

Cabot, John   33
Cadas   93
Cadiz   15, 18, 54
Calico   85, 108
Cambrian HMS   9 (Fig 1)
'Cambridge Flag'   48
Camperdown, Battle of   60, 89, 105 (note 119); Plates X, XIII
Canada   117
Canton   108
Cartagena   54
Cartel   108-9
Castile   53-6, 93
Cato   81 (Fig 93)
Cecil, Sir Edward   18
Centurion, HMS   22
Chappell, Reuben   40 (Fig 47)
Charles I, King of England and Scotland   16-19
– Royal Standard of: Plate I, number 2
Charles II, King of England and Scotland   19-22, 102 (note 46)
– Royal Standard of: Plate I, number 2
Charles III, King of Spain   105 (note 108)
Charles V, Emperor   53
Chatham   18, 19, 86-8 (Fig 96)
Chesapeake   50 (Figs 68-9), 89
China, Flags from: 89; Back cover

Church pennant   109
Cleirac, E   113
Clerk, A de   82 (Fig 94)
Cleveley, John (the Elder)   23
   (Fig 18), 25 (Fig 24)
Cloth of Gold, Field of   12-13
   (Fig 3)
Collingwood, Vice Admiral
   Cuthbert   30-1
Colonial flags   31, 47-8 (Fig 64)
Colours   18, 96, 97, 109 and see
   'Ensign'
Columbus, Christopher   53-4, 105
   (note 105)
Command, Flags of   108
- American   52
- British   10, 12-14, 17, 18-19, 21-5,
   27-8, 30-2 (Fig 31), 79, 89, 95, 98,
   99; Plates VII, XI
- Dutch   56-8; Plate XIII
- French   61-3
- Sizes of   86-8
Commercial Code of Signals   82
   (Fig 94), 84, Back endpaper
Commodore   25, 31-2, 52, 62, 98,
   99, 102 (note 48), 109
- Broad pennant   25, 30-2 (Figs 30-
   1), 62, 98, 99, 102 (note 48), 108;
   Plate III, number 28
- Shipping Company   39
Commonwealth period   19-20, 87,
   and see 'Dutch Wars'
Confederate States   51-2; Plate
   XIV, numbers 6-7
'Continental Colours'   48 (Fig 65);
   Plate XIV, number 1
Convenience, Flag of   109
Cornet   109
Cornwall, Arms of   93
Court martial   109
Courtesy ensign   35, 109
Crampton, W G   8, 32, 115
Crimean War   89
Cromwell, Oliver   19-20 (Fig 15),
   101 (note 32)
'Cross and harp' Flag   19, 101 (note
   33), 102 (note 37); Plate II,
   number 13
Crown   109
Crystal Stream   82 (Fig 94)
Cumberland Fleet   44
Cunard   39 (Fig 45), 42
Customs and Excise   40-1 (Figs 48-
   9), 97, 103 (note 78)
Cyclopedia (Rees)   41 (Fig 48)

Danckerts, C   115
Daunce, Sir John   93-4

Deane, Richard   77
Deface   109
Defiance, Flag of see 'Bloody Flag'
Delft   105 (note 114)
Denmark   95, 119; Plate XVI,
   number 32
Deptford   18
Desroches   114
Dip   109
Distinguishing flag   109
Distress   81 (Fig 93), 83, 109
Dockyards   85
- Chatham   18, 19, 86-8 (Fig 96)
- Deptford   18
- Portsmouth   18
Dönitz, Grossadmiral Karl   89, 91
   (Fig 104)
Downman, William   114; Plate IV
Downs, Distinction pennant
   for   24-5 (Fig 22)
Dragon   93-4
Drake, Sir Francis   14 (Fig 5), 15,
   33, 84, 85, 92, 100 (note 13), 103
   (note 63), 107 (note 150)
Drake, Rear Admiral Sir Francis
   Samuel   102-3 (note 52)
Dressing Ship   83-4 (Fig 95), 106
   (note 147)
Dudley, John, Viscount Lisle   13
Dugdale, Sir William   107 (note
   154)
Duncan, Admiral Viscount   89, and
   see 'Camperdown'
Dutch Wars   19-25 (Figs 13, 14,
   17), 56-8, 77, 85, 90
Dutton, TG   30 (Fig 30), 38 (Fig
   42)

East India Company
- British   36-7 (Figs 39, 40), 48, 82,
   103 (note 72)
- Dutch   56, 105 (note 114)
Edward VII, King of Great
   Britain   45 (Fig 59), 92
Elizabeth I, Queen of England   12-
   15, 36, 85, 86
- Royal Standard of: Plate I,
   number 1
Elizabeth II, Queen of Great
   Britain   89
'England expects ...'   82; Front
   endpaper
Ensign   10, 14, 17-19, 21 (Fig 16),
   22, 25, 26 (Fig 25), 28, 30, 31, 32,
   33, 36-7, 96-7, 98, 99
- American   47-52; Plate XIV,
   numbers 1-4, 6, 7

- Battle   108
- Blue   18, 31, 34, 45, 99; Plate II,
   number 21, Plate III, number 32
- British merchant   33-7, 97, 98,
   99; Plate II, numbers 17, 19, Plate
   III, number 31
- British naval   12-32 (Fig 25);
   Plates II, III
- Courtesy   35
- Dutch   57-8; Plate XV, numbers
   15, 16, 20
- French   60-4, Plate XVI, numbers
   22, 23, 26
- James II's   23 (Fig 19)
- Red   18-19, 25, 28, 31, 33-5, 47,
   97, 98, 99; Plate II, numbers 17, 19,
   Plate III, number 31
- Scottish   17 (Fig 10), 33; Plate II,
   number 18
- Signalling with   77, 78, 81
- Sizes of   86-8
- Spanish   53-6; Plate XIV,
   numbers 8, 10, Plate XV, numbers
   11, 13
- Striped   14-15 (Fig 6), 17-18, 33,
   36-7, 50-1, 77-8 (Figs 87-9), 100
   (notes 7, 14), 101 (note 27); Plate
   II, numbers 15, 16
- Upside down   81 (Fig 93), 83, 109
- White   18, 25, 28, 31, 34, 44-5, 87,
   99, 102 (note 49), 104 (note 83);
   Plate II, number 20, Plate III,
   number 30
Ensign Staff   28, 31, 88, 109
Essex, Earl of   15

Falkland Islands War   46
Falmouth   42, 104 (note 79)
False colours   109
Farley, Henry   101 (note 23)
Farnese, Arms of   54
Federal Steam Navigation Co   39
Ferdinand, King of Aragon   53, 54
Ferrol   54
Fighting Instructions   77-81, 88
Fimbriation   30, 109
Finch, Karen   101
Finial   109
First World War   32, 89, 91
Fisher, M   115
Fitzgerald, Arms of   30
Fixings   88, 107 (note 162)
'Flag' – defined   9, 95-6, 109
Flag Institute   113
Flag Officers   10, 27-8, 95, 98, 99,
   101 (note 19), 109, and see
   'Command, Flags of'
- of yacht clubs   45

Flag Research Center   113
Flags of All Nations   32, 40, 88, 113, 115
Flagships   12-14, 109, and see 'Flag Officer'
Flagstaff   88, 93 and see 'Ensign Staff', 'Jackstaff'
Flanders   53
Fleur-de-lis   12, 30, 54, 60-2
Flushing   58-9 (Figs 78, 80)
Fly   43 (Fig 55)
Fly   109-10
Foul anchor   102 (note 40), 110 and see 'Lord High Admiral'
Four Days Battle   57
Fournier, G   60
France   25, 28, 31, 60-4, (Figs 82-6), 89-90 (Figs 98, 99), 95, 117-8; Plate XVI, numbers 22-26
- Royal Arms of   12, 30, 54, 60-2, 90 (Fig 98), 100 (note 3)
Franklin, Benjamin   49
Frederick, Duke of York and Albany   Plate XII
Friesland   56, 114
Frigate Bay, Battle of   106 (note 126)
Frobisher, Martin   77
Funnel markings   39

'G' flag   111
Gaff   28, 110
Galley fleets   77
- French   62-3 (Fig 84)
- Spanish   54
- Venetian   54
Garter, Order of   111
Generals at Sea   19, 77, 101 (note 35)
George I, King of Great Britain
- Royal Standard of   Plate I, number 5
George II, King of Great Britain
- Royal Standard of   Plate I, number 5
George III, King of Great Britain
- Royal Standard of   Plate I, numbers 5-7
George IV, King of Great Britain
- Royal Standard of   Plate I, number 7
Germany   32, 89-91 (Figs 103, 104), 118, Plate XVI, numbers 28-30
Gibraltar   56 (Fig 75)
Gipkyn, John   101 (note 23)
Globe   104 (note 91)

'Glorious First of June', Battle of (1794)   27, 62, 87, 89, 90 (Fig 98), 107 (note 165); Plate VII
Gold, use of   12, 85, 93-4
Golden Fleece, Order of   53, 105 (note 108)
Golden Hind   84, 103 (note 63)
Granada   53
Graydon, George   106 (note 133)
Graydon, John   47, 102 (note 44), 114
Great Britain   35
'Great Union Flag'   48
Great Western   35
Green's of Blackwall   39 (Fig 44)
Greenwich Hospital   32 (Fig 32), 89, and see 'National Maritime Museum'
Greenwood, Jonathan   78-9 (Fig 90)
Greyhound   94
Guienne   93
'Guinea Jack'   36 (Figs 37-8)
Gyronny Flags   57 (Fig 77), 59, 110; Plate XV, number 21

Half-masting   110
Halyard   88, 110
Hapsburg, Philip of   53
Harp   16, 19, 21, 102 (note 46)
Havana   89
Hawkins, Sir John   33, 85
Heather, W   115
Hebrus, HMS   90 (Fig 99)
Henri Grace à Dieu, HMS   12-13 (Fig 4), 85, 86, 93-4
Henry VIII, King of England   12-13. 14, 86, 93-4, 100 (note 4)
Henry, HMS   24 (Fig 21)
Heraldry Society   113
Hesman, G   114
Heyward, William   93
Hogue, Battle of La   106 (note 126)
Hoist   110
Holland   56, 59, 105 (note 117), and see 'Netherlands'
Holman, Francis   43 (Fig 55), 49 (Fig 66), 51
Homewood, Mr   101 (note 35)
Hood, Samuel Viscount   81, 102-3 (note 52)
Hood, Thomas   101 (note 20)
Hopkins, Esek   48
Hopkinson, Francis   49
House flag   10, 36-9, 110, 119.20
Howard of Effingham, Lord   15, 16 (Fig 8), 101 (notes 18, 21)

Howe, Admiral of the Fleet Earl   28, 80-1, 87, 88, 89; Plate VII

Iconoclasm   12, 47, 100 (note 7)
Imperial War Museum   92
Inglefield clip   88, 110
Instructions   77-81 (Fig 87), 88
International Code of Signals   84, 88
Ireland   16, 19, 24, 102 (note 46), 103 (note 55)
Iron Duke, HMS   91 (Fig 101)
Isabella, Queen of Castile   53, 54
Italy   118

Jack   10, 17, 25, 33-4, 96, 110
- American   52; Plate XIV, number 5
- British Merchant   34-5 (Figs 33-6), 40 (Fig 47), 47, 98, 99, 103 (note 66)
- British Naval   See 'Union Jack'
- Dutch   59-60; Plate XV, number 11
- Etymology of   110
- French   62; Plate XVI, number 24
- Privateer   40, 43-4 (Fig 56), 97, 98
- Sizes of   87-8
- Spanish   54, 56; Plate XV, number 14
Jackstaff   10, 17, 88, 96, 109, 110
James I, King of England and Scotland   14-16
- Royal Standard of   16, 101 (note 20); Plate I, number 2
James II, King of England and Scotland   19, 22, 77 (Fig 87), 102 (note 44)
- Ensign of   22-3 (Fig 19)
- Royal Standard of: Plate I, number 2
James, Duke of York   77, and see 'James II'
Jellicoe, Admiral of the Fleet Earl   91 (Fig 101)
Jersey   103 (note 55)
Jervis, Admiral of the Fleet John, Earl St Vincent   81
'Johnson, Captain Charles'   45 (Fig 60), 104 (note 87)
'Jolly Roger'   46, 104 (note 89), 110
Jones, John Paul   48, 50-1
'Juana the Mad'   53

Justice, A   115
Jutland, Battle of   32, 91

Katherine of Aragon   12
Kempenfelt, Rear Admiral
   Richard   80
King's Colour   See 'Queen's
   Colour'
Kneller, Sir Godfrey   92 (Fig 105)
Knight, Sergeant John   100 (note
   8), 101 (note 20), 102 (note 46)
Kronstadt   92 (Fig 102)

Launching flags   22-3 (Fig 18), 110
Laurie, R H ·   115, Plate VIII
Le Breton   52 (Fig 71)
Le Gras, A   115
Lens, B   114; Plate VI
Leon   53-6, 105 (note 108)
Lepanto, Battle of   54, 105 (note
   106)
Letters of marque (mart)   See
   'Privateer'
Levant Company   36
Lexington   48-9 (Fig 65)
Liberty   60 (Fig 81), 89; Plate XV,
   number 20
Life-boats   110
Linen   85, 89
Lion   53-6, 58-60, 94, 105 (note
   117), and see 'Royal Arms'
Lisle, Viscount   13
Liverpool   37, 103 (note 73)
Livery colours   14, 100 (notes 4,
   14), 110
Lloyd's Book of House Flags   39
Lloyd's Register   84
Lloyd's Register of Yachts   104 (note
   84)
Lord High Admiral   13-14, 15, 18,
   21, 22, 95, 97
– Anchor Flag of (Admiralty
   Flag)   22, 32 (Fig 32) 102 (notes
   40, 43, 44), Plate I, number 9
Louis XIV, King of France   61-2
Lowestoft, Battle of   22, 57

Madeross   36 (Fig 38)
Mariner's Mirror   101 (note 18)
Marlborough, HMS   63 (Fig 85)
Marryat, Captain Frederick   34, 38
   (Fig 42), 83-4, 88
Mary Rose, HMS   12-13 (Fig 4)

Massachusetts   47, 49
Mayflower   15-17, 33
Medici, Arms of   54
Medway barge flags   92
Mercantile Navy List   84
Merchant Shipping Act   34
Merchant ships, Flags of
– American   51-2; Plate XIV,
   number 3
– British   33-9, 47, 98, 99; Plate II,
   numbers 17, 19; Plate III, number
   31
– Dutch   56-60
– French   60-2 (Fig 82)
– Spanish   54-60; Plate XV,
   number 11
See also 'House flags'
Merrimack   52 (Fig 71)
Millan, J   78-9 (Fig 89), 115
Mitchell, Thomas   27 (Fig 26)
Monck, George, Earl of
   Albemarle   77
Monitor   52 (Fig 71)
Montagne   62
Morro Castle   89-90 (Fig 97)
Morse Code   110
Mountagu, Edward   20
Moutton, J   113

Name pennant   39, 40 (Fig 47)
Napoleon   64, 89
Naseby   20, 22
National Maritime Museum   11,
   58, 79
– Flags at   19, 45 (Fig 59), 49 (Fig
   67), 50 (Fig 68), 56 (Figs 75, 76),
   60 (Fig 81), 85, 87, 89-92 (Figs 98-
   104); Plates VII, XI, XII, XIII
Naval Historical (formerly
   Admiralty) Library   113, 115,
   116, 117
Navarre   53, 56
Navy Board   40, 41 (Fig 48), 97
Nelson, Vice Admiral Viscount   27-
   31, 89
– Signals at Trafalgar   80-2

Neptune François   55 (Fig 74), 57
   (Fig 77), 58 (Fig 78), 61 (Fig 83),
   114
Netherlands   33, 56-60, 89, 95,
   118; Plate XV, numbers 15-21; and
   see 'Dutch Wars'
New England   47 (Figs 62, 63)
Newport, Rhode Island   46
Nile, Battle of the   27, 28
Norie, J W   34, 115

Northesk, Rear Admiral theEarl
   of   31
Number, Make her   83, 110
Numerary flags   80-4
Nylon   85

Orange, House of   24, 56, 85
Ordnance, Board of   40, 41 (Fig
   48), 97, 103 (note 76)

'P' flag   84, 108
Packets   41-2, 104 (note 79)
Pasco, John   82
Passebon, H S de   63 (Fig 84)
Pavise   12
Payne, J   18 (Fig 12)
Peak   28, 110
Pencel   12, 93-4
Pendant   110 and see 'Pennant'
Pennant   10, 12, 14, 19, 21-2, 25,
   31, 33, 34, 35, 88, 96, 97, 98, 99,
   102 (notes 39, 48, 50), 110
– American   52, 104 (note 101)
– Blue   Plate III, number 26
– Broad   25, 30 (Fig 30), 31-2, 52,
   62, 98, 99, 102 (note 48) 108, Plate
   III, number 28
– Budgee   25 (Fig 23), 102 (note 48)
– Church   109
– Commissioning   10, 110
– Common (Union)   22, 25, 31, 102
   (note 50), 103 (note 60); Plate III,
   number 23
– Customs and Excise   40-1
– Distinction   24-5 (Fig 22)
– Dutch   56-8, 102 (note 39); Plate
   XV, number 19
– East India Co   36-7 (Fig 39), 103
   (note 72)
– Fixings of   88
– French   61-4, Plate XVI,
   number 25
– Homeward-bound   110
– Name   39, 40 (Fig 47)
– Packet   42
– Paying-off   110
– Red   Plate III, number 24
– Royal Mail   42 (Figs 51, 52)
– Senior officer's   99, 102 (note 48),
   111
– Sizes of
   – English   86-8
   – French   62
– Spelling of   110
– White   31, 99; Plate III, number
   25. See also 'Streamer'
Pennsylvania   49

Pepys, Samuel 19, 20, 33, 36-7, 85, 87, 92 (Fig 105), 100 (notes 1, 8, 16), 101 (note 31), 102 (notes 38, 44)
Perrin, W G 11
Petra Sancta, S 10-11 (Fig 2)
Philip II, King of Spain 53, and see 'Armada'
Philip IV, King of Spain 54
Phillips, T 23 (Fig 17), 105 (note 116)
Pilot flag 111
Pilot jack 34-5 (Figs 34, 36), 40 (Fig 47), 99, 103 (note 66), 110
Pirates 45-6
Pocock, Nicholas 11, 63 (Fig 85), 102 (note 51), 104 (note 99), 106 (note 126)
Polar flags 92
Polyester 86
Pomegranate 12, 93
Pope, C M 89
Popham, Captain Sir Home 81-3
Porpoise 81 (Fig 93)
Portcullis 12, 40-1
Portsmouth 18
– Battle of 12-13 (Fig 4)
Portugal 53, 118; Plate XVI, number 27
Post Office 41-2 (Figs 50-2)
Pratique 84, 111
Press gang 98
'Prince flag' 56; Plate XV, numbers 15, 16
Prince of Wales 16, 45 (Fig 59), 92
Prince Royal, HMS 17 (Fig 11)
Private ship 111
Privateer 33, 42-4 (Fig 57), 97, 98
– Jack 43-4 (Fig 56), 97, 98, 108
Prize flags 45, 92
Puritans see 'Iconoclasm'

'Q' flag 84, 111
Quarantine flag 84, 111
Quartering 111
Queen Charlotte, HMS 87, 89; Plate VII; and see 'Glorious First of June'
'Queen's Colour' 111
Queen's Regulations 25, 32, 34, 40, 42, 106 (note 147), 109, 111, 117

Racing flags 45
'Ragged cross' 53-6 (Figs 74-5), 105 (note 104); Plate XIV, number 8

Raleigh, HMS 30 (Fig 30)
Rattlesnake 48, 49, 104 (note 102)
Red flag see 'Bloody flag'
Religious flags 12, 53-4, 105 (note 107)
Repeating frigates 111
Revenue cutters 40, 103 (note 78), 111
Richardson, J M and G B 84
'Right of the Flag' 17, 33, 95
Rijksmuseum 36, 53, 85, 87, 90, 105 (note 116)
Roberts, Bartholomew 45-6 (Fig 60)
Robinson, M S 8, 58, 105 (note 116)
Rodney, Admiral Lord 28, 80
Roebuck, HMS 49 (Fig 66), 51
Roome, John 106 (note 140)
Rose 12, 18, 93
Ross, Betsy 49
Rotterdam 56, 58, 102 (note 44), 105 (notes 116, 119)
Royal Africa Co. 36 (Figs 37-8)
Royal Arms
– British 10, 12, 15 (Fig 7), 33, 53, 86, 93, 100 (note 3), 101 (note 18), 103 (note 57), 113; Plate I, numbers 1-8; and see 'Standard'
– French 12, 30, 54, 60-2, 90 (Fig 99), 100 (note 3)
– Spanish 53-6, 89-90 (Fig 97), 93, 105 (note 108); Plate XIV, numbers 9, 10; Plate XV, number 13
Royal George, HMS 80
Royal Mail pennant 42 (figs 51-2)
Royal Naval Reserve 31, 34, 99; Plate III, number 11
Royal Navy 12-32, 77-82, 85-8, 89
Royal Prince, HMS Front cover
Royal Sovereign, HMS 30-1
Royal Standard 10, 111 and see 'Standard'
Royal Thames Yacht Club 44, 104 (note 82)
Royal United Service Museum 89
Royal Yachts 32, 45, 89, 92, 102 (notes 42, 44, 46), 104 (note 83)
Royal Yacht Squadron 44-5 (Fig 58)
Rupert, Prince 22
Russia, Flags of 89, 91 (Fig 102)
Ruyter, Admiral Michiel De 57, 105 (note 116)

Sailing Instructions 77-81 (Fig 87), 88

Sailmaker, Isaac 37 (Fig 40), 103 (note 72)
Sails, Decoration on 12, 100 (note 5)
Saints
– Arms of 12
– Images of 12, 100 (note 7)
– St Andrew, Cross of 12, 16, 17 (Fig 10), 30, 33, 95-6, 101 (note 21); Plate I, number 11
– St Edward the Confessor 93, 100 (note 6)
– Saint Esprit, Order of 62
– St George, Cross of 12-32 (passim; Fig 31), 33-4, 38, 47, 60, 85, 93-4, 95-6, 98, 100 (note 14), 101 (note 21); Plate I, number 10
– 'Saint George's jack' 34 (Fig 33), 47, 98
– St James of Compostela 53
– St Michael, Order of 62
– St Patrick, Cross of 24, 28 (Fig 27), 30, 103 (note 55)
Saints, Battle of the 27-8 (Fig 26), 80, 102 (note 51)
Salem (Massachusetts) 47
Salmon, Robert 103 (note 73)
Saltire 12, 16, 24, 28 (Fig 27), 30, 33, 95, 101 (note 21), 103 (note 55), 111; Plate I, number 11
– Raguly 53-6 (Figs 74, 75), 105 (note 104); Plate XIV, number 8
San Augustin 14 (Fig 5)
San Ildefonso 89
Say 106-7 (note 148)
Scheveningen, Battle of 19, 20 (Fig 14), 101 (Notes 34, 36), 105 (note 116)
Scotland 12, 16, 19, 30, 33, 95, 101 (note 21)
– Admiral of 22, 102 (note 44)
– Ensign of 17 (Fig 10), 33; Plate II, number 18
– Union Flag of 16-17 (Fig 10), 101 (note 21), 115 (Fig 107)
Second World War 52, 89, 91 (Fig 104)
Semaphore 82, 111
Serapis HMS 50-1
Serres, J T 9 (Fig 1)
Shannon, HMS 50 (Fig 69), 89
Sicily 53
Signal books 78-84, 111
Signalling 77-84
– Commercial Code 82 (Fig 94); Back endpaper
– International Code 84, 88; Back endpaper
– Marryat's Code 34, 38 (Fig 42), 83-4, 88; Back endpaper